Dimensions of Ethnicity

A Series of Selections from the
Harvard Encyclopedia of American Ethnic Groups

Stephan Thernstrom, *Editor*
Ann Orlov, *Managing Editor*
Oscar Handlin, *Consulting Editor*

THE POLITICS OF ETHNICITY

MICHAEL WALZER
EDWARD T. KANTOWICZ
JOHN HIGHAM
MONA HARRINGTON

The Belknap Press of
Harvard University Press
Cambridge, Massachusetts
London, England
1982

Printed in the United States of America

Library of Congress Cataloging in Publication Data

Main entry under title:

The Politics of ethnicity.

    (Dimensions of ethnicity)
    Selections from the Harvard Encyclopedia of American ethnic groups.
    Bibliography: p.
    1. Ethnic groups—Political activity—Addresses, essays, lectures.
2. United States—Politics and government—20th century—Addresses,
essays, lectures. 3. Pluralism (Social sciences)—Addresses, essays, lectures.
4. Voting—United States—Addresses, essays, lectures. 5. Political parties—
United States—Addresses, essays, lectures. I. Walzer, Michael. II. Series.
E184.A1P64 1982   306'.2   82-6128
ISBN 0-674-68753-1 (pbk.)   AACR2

Foreword

Ethnicity is a central theme—perhaps the central theme—of American history. From the first encounters between Englishmen and Indians at Jamestown down to today's "boat people," the interplay between peoples of differing national origins, religions, and races has shaped the character of our national life. Although scholars have long recognized this fact, in the past two decades they have paid it more heed than ever before. The result has been an explosive increase in research on America's complex ethnic mosaic. Examination of a recent bibliography of doctoral dissertations on ethnic themes written between 1899 and 1972 reveals that no less than half of them appeared in the years 1962–1972. The pace of inquiry has not slackened since then; it has accelerated.

The extraordinary proliferation of literature on ethnicity and ethnic groups made possible—and necessary—an effort to take stock. An authoritative, up-to-date synthesis of the current state of knowledge in the field was called for. *The Harvard Encyclopedia of American Ethnic Groups*, published by the Harvard University Press in 1980, is such a synthesis. It provides entries by leading scholars on the origins, history, and present situation of the more than 100 ethnic groups that make up the population of the United States, and 29 thematic essays on a wide range of ethnic topics. As one reviewer said, the volume is "a kind of *summa ethnica* of our time."

I am pleased that some of the most interesting and valuable articles in the encyclopedia are now available to a wider audience through inexpensive paperback editions such as this one. These essays will be an excellent starting point for anyone in search of deeper understanding of who the American people are and how they came to be that way.

Stephan Thernstrom

Contents

The Politics of Ethnicity

1
PLURALISM
IN POLITICAL
PERSPECTIVE

Democracy and Nationalism

Most political theorists, from the time of the Greeks onward, have assumed the national or ethnic homogeneity of the communities about which they wrote. Prior
to the work of Rousseau, theory was never explicitly
nationalist, but the assumption of a common language,
history, or religion underlay most of what was said
about political practices and institutions. Hence, the
only empire systematically defended in the great tradition of political theory was the Christian empire of the
Middle Ages: one religious communion, it was argued,
made one political community. The religiously mixed
empires of ancient and modern times, by contrast, had
no theoretical defenders, only publicists and apolo-
gists. Political thinking has been dominated by the
Greece of Pericles, not of Alexander; by republican
Rome, not the Roman empire; by Venice and Holland,
not the Europe of the Hapsburgs. Even liberal writers,
ready enough to acknowledge a plurality of interests,

were strikingly unready for a plurality of cultures. One people made one state. The argument of the authors of *The Federalist Papers* (1787–1788) may be taken here to sum up a long tradition of thought. The Americans, John Jay wrote, were a people "descended from the same ancestors, speaking the same language, professing the same religion, attached to the same principles of government, very similar in their manners and customs." Surely a "band of brethren" so united "should never be split into a number of unsocial, jealous, and alien sovereignties."

Jay's description was only very roughly true of America in 1787, and clearly the maxim *One people, one state* has, throughout human history, been honored most often in the breach. Most often, brethren have been divided among alien sovereignties and forced to coexist with strangers under an alien sovereign. National and ethnic pluralism has been the rule, not the exception. The theoretical preference for cultural unity existed for centuries alongside dynastic and imperial institutions that made for disunity. Only in the late 18th and 19th centuries was the old assumption of homogeneity, reinforced by new democratic commitments, transformed into a practical demand for separation and independence. Underlying that demand were two powerful ideas: first, that free government was only possible under conditions of cultural unity; second, that free individuals would choose if they could to live with their own kind, that is, to join political sovereignty to national or ethnic community. No doubt these ideas could be challenged. Marx and his followers emphatically denied that they were true, arguing that conceptions of "kind" were ultimately based on class rather than ethnic distinctions. But the two ideas had the support of a long intellectual tradition, and they happily supported one another. They suggested that democracy and self-determination led to the same political arrangements that their effective exercise required: the replacement of empires by national states.

In practice, this replacement took two very different forms. The new nationalist politics was first of all expressed in the demand for the unification of peoples divided—as were the Germans, Italians, and Slavs—among the old empires and a variety of petty principalities. Nationalist leaders aimed initially at large states and at a broad (pan-German or pan-Slavic) definition of cultural homogeneity. Yugoslavia and Czechoslovakia are products of this first nationalism which, though it entailed the breakup of empires, was still a politics of composition, not of division. The Zionist "ingathering" of Jews from Europe and the Orient has the same character. Roughly similar groups were to be welded together, on the model of the prenationalist unifications of France and Britain.

This early nation-building was hardly a failure, but the clear tendency of nationalism more recently has been to challenge not only the old empires, especially the colonial empires, but also the composite nation-states. Neither the oldest states (France, Britain) nor the newest (Pakistan, Nigeria) have been safe from such challenges. Secession rather than unification is the current theme. International society today is marked by the proliferation of states, so that "the majority of the members of the U.N.," as Eric Hobsbawm has written, "is soon likely to consist of the late-twentieth-century (republican) equivalents of Saxe-Coburg-Gotha and Schwarzburg-Sonderhausen." Important transformations of the world economy have opened the way for this process: the rules of viability have radically changed since the 19th century. But the process also represents an extraordinary triumph for the principle of self-determination—with the collective self increasingly defined in ways that reflect the actual diversity of mankind.

Confronted with this diversity, every putative nation-state is revealed as an ancient or modern composition. Self-determination looks to be a principle of endless applicability, and the appearance of new states a process of indefinite duration. If the process is to be cut short, it is unlikely to be by denying the principle—for it appears today politically undeniable—but rather by administering it in moderate doses. Thus autonomy may be an alternative to independence, loosening the bonds of the composite state, a way to avoid their fracture. Instead of sovereignty, national and ethnic groups may opt for decentralization, devolution, and federalism; these are not incompatible with self-determination, and they may be especially appropriate for groups of people who share some but not all of the characteristics of a distinct historical community and who retain a strong territorial base. Whether composite states can survive as federations is by no means certain, but it is unlikely that they can survive in any other way—not, at least, if they remain committed (even if only formally) to democratic government or to some sort of social egalitarianism.

Democracy and equality have proven to be the great solvents. In the old empires, the elites of conquered nations tended to assimilate to the dominant culture. They sent their children to be educated by their conquerors; they learned an alien language; they came to see their own culture as parochial and inferior. But ordinary men and women did not assimilate, and when they were mobilized, first for economic and then for political activity, they turned out to have deep national and ethnic loyalties. Mobilization made for conflict, not only with the dominant groups, but also with other submerged peoples. For centuries, perhaps, different nations had lived in peace, side by side, under imperial rule. Now that they had to rule themselves, they found that they could do so (peacefully) only among themselves, adjusting political lines to cultural boundaries.

So the assumptions of the theoretical tradition have proven true. Self-government has tended to produce relatively homogeneous communities and has been fully successful only within such communities. The great exception to this rule is the United States. At the same time, the Marxist argument, the most significant challenge to traditional wisdom, has proven wrong. Nowhere have class loyalties overridden the commitment to national and ethnic groups. Today, the Soviet Union resembles nothing so much as the empire of the Romanovs: a multinational state held together chiefly by force. Conceivably, if the "national question" were ever solved, if the existence and continued development of historical communities were guaranteed (as Lenin argued they should be), new patterns of alliance and cooperation might emerge. But for the moment, it must be said that politics follows nationality, wherever politics is free. Pluralism in the strong sense—*One state, many peoples*—is possible only under tyrannical regimes.

American Exceptionalism

Except in the United States. Here too, of course, there are conquered and incorporated peoples—Indian tribes, Mexicans—who stood in the path of American expansion, and there are forcibly transported peoples —the blacks—brought to this country as slaves and subjected to a harsh and continuous repression. But the pluralist system within which these groups have only recently begun to organize and act is not primarily the product of their experience. Today, the United States can only be understood as a multiracial society. But the minority races were politically impotent and socially invisible during much of the time when American pluralism was taking shape—and the shape it took was not determined by their presence or by their repression.

In contrast to the Old World, where pluralism had its origins in conquest and dynastic alliance, pluralism in the New World originated in individual and familial migration. The largest part of the U.S. population was formed by the addition of individuals, one by one, filtered through the great port cities. Though the boundaries of the new country, like those of every other country, were determined by war and diplomacy, it was immigration that determined the character of its inhabitants—and falsified John Jay's account of their unity. The United States was not an empire; its pluralism was that of an immigrant society, and that means that nationality and ethnicity never acquired a stable territorial base. Different peoples gathered in different parts of the country, but they did so by individual choice, clustering for company, with no special tie to the land on which they lived. The Old World call for self-determination had no resonance here: the immigrants (except for the black slaves) had come voluntarily and did not have to be forced to stay (indeed, many of them returned home each year), nor did groups of immigrants have any basis for or any reason for secession. The only significant secessionist movement in U.S. history, though it involved a region with a distinctive culture, did not draw upon nationalist passions of the sort that have figured in European wars.

But if the immigrants became Americans one by one as they arrived and settled, they did so only in a political sense: they became U.S. citizens. In other respects, culturally, religiously, even for a time linguistically, they remained Germans and Swedes, Poles, Jews, and Italians. With regard to the first immigrants, the Anglo-Americans, politics still followed nationality: because they were one people, they made one state. But with the newer immigrants, the process was reversed. Because they were citizens of one state—so it was commonly thought—they would become one people. Nationality would follow politics, as it presumably had in earlier times, when the peoples of the modern world were first formed. For a while, however, perhaps for a long while, the United States would be a country composed of many peoples, sharing residence and citizenship only, without a common history or culture.

In such circumstances, the only emotion that made for unity was patriotism. Hence the efforts of the late 19th and early 20th centuries to intensify patriotic feeling, to make a religion out of citizenship. "The voting booth is the temple of American institutions," Supreme Court Justice David Brewer wrote in 1900. "No single tribe or family is chosen to watch the sacred fires burning on its altars . .   Each of us is a priest." The rise of ethnic political machines and bloc voting, however, must have made the temple seem disturbingly like a sectarian conventicle. Few people believed politics to be a sufficient ground for national unity. Patriotism was essentially a holding action, while the country waited for the stronger solidarity of nationalism. Whether the process of Americanization was described as a gradual assimilation to Anglo-American culture or as the creation of an essentially new culture in the crucible of citizenship, its outcome was thought to be both necessary and inevitable: the immigrants would one day constitute a single people. This was the deeper meaning that the slogan *From many, one* (*E pluribus unum*) took on in the context of mass immigration. The only alternatives, as the history of the Old World taught, were divisiveness, turmoil, and repression.

The fear of divisiveness, or simply of difference, periodically generated outbursts of anti-immigrant feeling among the first immigrants and their descendants. Restraint of all further immigration was one goal of these "nativist" campaigns; the second goal was a more rapid Americanization of the "foreigners" already here. But what did Americanization entail? Many of the foreigners were already naturalized citizens. Now they were to be naturalized again, not politically but culturally. It is worth distinguishing this second naturalization from superficially similar campaigns in the old European empires. Russification, for example, was also a cultural program, but it was aimed at intact and rooted communities, at nations that, with the exception of the Jews, were established on lands they had occupied for many centuries. None of the peoples who were to be Russified could have been trusted with citizenship in a free Russia. Given the chance, they would have opted for secession and independence. That was why Russification was so critical: political means were required to overcome national differences. And the use of those means produced the predictable democratic response that politics should follow nationality, not oppose it. In the United States, by contrast, Americanization was aimed at peoples far more susceptible to cultural change, for they were not only uprooted; they had uprooted themselves. Whatever the pressures that had driven them to the New World, they had chosen to come, while others like themselves, in their own families, had chosen to remain. And as a reward for their choice, the immigrants had been offered citizenship, a gift that many eagerly accepted. Though nativists feared or pretended to fear the politics of the newcomers, the fact is that the men and women who were to be Americanized were already, many of them, patriotic Americans.

Because of these differences, the response of the immigrants to cultural naturalization was very different from that of their counterparts in the Old World. They were in many cases acquiescent, ready to make themselves over, even as the nativists asked. This was especially true in the area of language: there has been no longterm or successful effort to maintain the original language of the newcomers as anything more than a second language in the United States. The vitality of Spanish in the Southwest today, though it probably results from the continued large-scale influx of Mexican immigrants, suggests a possible exception to this rule. If these immigrants do not distribute themselves around the country, as other groups have done, a state like New Mexico might provide the first arena for sustained linguistic conflict in the United States. Until now, however, in a country where many languages are spoken, there has been remarkably little conflict. English is and has always been acknowledged as the public language of the American republic, and no one has tried to make any other language the basis for regional autonomy or secession. When the immigrants did resist Americanization, struggling to hold on to old identities and old customs, their resistance took a new form. It was not a demand that politics follow nationality, but rather that politics be separated from nationality—as it was already separated from religion. It was not a demand for national liberation, but for ethnic pluralism.

The Practice of Pluralism

As a general intellectual tendency, pluralism in the early 20th century was above all a reaction against the doctrine of sovereignty. In its different forms—syndicalist, guild socialist, regionalist, autonomist—it was directed against the growing power and the far-reaching claims of the modern state. But ethnic pluralism as it developed in the United States cannot plausibly be characterized as an antistate ideology. Its advocates did not challenge the authority of the federal government; they did not defend states' rights; they were not drawn to any of the forms of European corporatism. Their central assertion was that U.S. politics, as it was, did not require cultural homogeneity; it rested securely enough on democratic citizenship. What had previously been understood as a temporary condition was now described as if it might be permanent. The United States was, and could safely remain, a country composed of many peoples, a "nation of nationalities," as Horace Kallen called it. Indeed, this was the destiny of America: to maintain the diversity of the Old World in a single state, without persecution or repression. Not only *From many, one,* but also *Within one, many.*

Marxism was the first major challenge to the traditional argument for national homogeneity; ethnic pluralism is the second. Although the early pluralists were by no means radicals, and never advocated social transformation, there is a certain sense in which their denial of conventional wisdom goes deeper than that of the Marxists. For the Marxist argument suggests that the future socialist state (before it withers away) will rest upon the firm base of proletarian unity. And like each previous ruling class, the proletariat is expected to produce a hegemonic culture, of which political life would be merely one expression. Pluralists, on the other hand, imagined a state unsupported by either unity or hegemony. No doubt, they were naïve not to recognize the existence of a single economic system and then of a culture reflecting dominant economic values. But their argument is far-reaching and important even if it is taken to hold only that in addition to this common culture, overlaying it, radically diversifying its impact, there is a world of ethnic multiplicity. The effect on the theory of the state is roughly the same with or without the economic understanding: politics must still create the (national) unity it was once thought merely to mirror. And it must create unity without denying or repressing multiplicity.

The early pluralist writers—theorists like Horace Kallen and Randolph Bourne, popularizers like Louis Adamic—did not produce a fully satisfying account of this creative process or of the ultimately desirable relation between the political one and the cultural many. Their arguments rarely advanced much beyond glowing description and polemical assertion. Drawing heavily upon 19th-century romanticism, they insisted upon the intrinsic value of human difference and, more plausibly and importantly, upon the deep need of

human beings for historically and communally struc-
tured forms of life. Every kind of regimentation, every
kind of uniformity was alien to them. They were the
self-appointed guardians of a society of groups, a society resting upon stable families (despite the disrup-
tions of the immigrant experience), tied into, bearing,
and transmitting powerful cultural traditions. At the
same time, their politics was little more than an unexa-
mined liberalism. Freedom for individuals, they were
certain, was all that was necessary to uphold group
identification and ethnic flourishing. They had surprisingly little to say about how the different groups were
to be held together in a single political order, what citizenship might mean in a pluralist society, whether
state power should ever be used on behalf of groups, or
what social activities should be assigned to or left to
groups. The practical meaning of ethnic pluralism has
been hammered out, is still being hammered out, in
the various arenas of political and social life. Little theoretical justification exists for any particular outcome.

The best way to understand pluralism, then, is to
look at what its protagonists have done or tried to do.
Ethnic self-assertion in the United States has been the
functional equivalent of national liberation in other
parts of the world. What are the actual functions that it
serves? There are three that seem critically important.
First of all, the defense of ethnicity against cultural naturalization: Kallen's pluralism, worked out in a period
of heightened nativist agitation and political persecution (see his *Culture and Democracy in the United States*,
1924), is primarily concerned with upholding the right

of the new immigrants, as individuals, to form themselves into cultural communities and maintain their foreign ways. Kallen joins the early-20th-century American *kulturkampf* as the advocate of cultural permissiveness. Train citizens, but leave nationality alone! The argument, so far as it is developed, is largely negative in character, and so it fits easily into the liberal paradigm. But Kallen is convinced that the chief product of a liberal society will not be individual selfhood but collective identity. Here surely he was right, or at least partly right. How many private wars, parallel to his intellectual campaign, have been fought on behalf of such identities—in schools, bureaucracies, corporations—against the pressures of Americanization! Most often, when individual men and women insist on "being themselves," they are in fact defending a self they share with others. Sometimes, of course, they succumb and learn to conform to standardized versions of New World behavior. Or they wait, frightened and passive, for organizational support: a league against defamation, a committee for advancement, and so on. When such organizations go to work, the pluralist form of the struggle is plain to see, even if legal and moral arguments continue to focus on individual rights.

The second function of ethnic assertiveness is more positive in character: the celebration of this or that identity. Celebration is critical to every national and ethnic movement because both foreign conquest and immigration to foreign lands work, though in different ways, to undermine communal confidence. Immigration involves a conscious rejection of the old country and then, often, of oneself as a product of the old country. A new land requires a new life, new ways of life. But in learning the new ways, the immigrant is slow, awkward, a greenhorn, quickly outpaced by his own children. He is likely to feel inferior, and his children are likely to confirm the feeling. But this sense of inferiority, so painful to him, is also a disaster for them. It cuts them adrift in a world where they are never likely to feel entirely at home. At some point, among themselves, or among their children (the second American generation), a process of recovery begins. Ethnic celebration is a feature of that process. It has a general and a particular form: the celebration of diversity itself and then of the history and culture of a particular group. The first of these, it should be stressed, would be meaningless without the second, for the first is abstract and the second concrete. Pluralism has in itself no powers of survival; it depends upon energy, enthusiasm, commitment within the component groups; it cannot outlast the particularity of cultures and creeds. From the standpoint of the liberal state, particularity is a matter of individual choice, and pluralism nothing more than toleration. From the standpoint of the individual, it is probably something else, for men and women mostly "choose" the culture and creed to which they were born—even if, after conquest and immigration, they have to be born again.

The third function of ethnic assertiveness is to build and sustain the reborn community—to create institutions, gain control of resources, and provide educational and welfare services. As with nation-building, this is hard work, but there is a difficulty peculiar to ethnic groups in a pluralist society: such groups do not have coercive authority over their members. Indeed, they do not have members in the same way that the state has citizens; they have no guaranteed population. Though they are historical communities, they must function as if they were voluntary associations. They must make ethnicity a cause, like prohibition or universal suffrage; they must persuade people to "ethnicize" rather than Americanize themselves. The advocates of religious ethnicity—German Lutherans, Irish Catholics, Jews, and so on—have probably been most successful in doing this. But any group that hopes to survive must commit itself to the same pattern of activity—winning support, raising money, building schools, community centers, and old-age homes.

On the basis of some decades of experience, one can reasonably argue that ethnic pluralism is entirely compatible with the existence of a unified republic. Kallen would have said that it is simply the expression of democracy in the sphere of culture. It is, however, an unexpected expression: the American republic is very different from that described, for example, by Montesquieu and Rousseau. It lacks the intense political fellowship, the commitment to public affairs, that they thought necessary. "The better the constitution of a state is," wrote Rousseau, "the more do public affairs encroach on private in the minds of the citizens. Private affairs are even of much less importance, because the aggregate of the common happiness furnishes a greater proportion of that of each individual, so that there is less for him to seek in particular cares." This is an unlikely description unless ethnic culture and religious belief are closely interwoven with political activity (as Rousseau insisted they should be). It certainly misses the reality of the American republic, where both have been firmly relegated to the private sphere. The emotional life of U.S. citizens is lived mostly in private —which is not to say in solitude, but in groups considerably smaller than the community of all citizens. Americans are communal in their private affairs, individualist in their politics. Society is a collection of groups; the state is an organization of individual citizens. And society and state, though they constantly interact, are formally distinct. For support and comfort and a sense of belonging, men and women look to their groups; for freedom and mobility, they look to the state.

Still, democratic participation does bring group members into the political arena where they are likely to discover common interests. Why has this not caused radical divisiveness, as in the European empires? It certainly has made for conflict, sometimes of a frightening sort, but always within limits set by the nonterritorial and socially indeterminate character of the immigrant communities and by the sharp divorce of state and ethnicity. No single group can hope to capture the state and turn it into a nation-state. Members of the group are citizens only as Americans, not as Germans, Italians, Irishmen, or Jews. Politics forces them into alliances and coalitions; and democratic politics, because it recognizes each citizen as the equal of every other, without regard to ethnicity, fosters a unity of individuals alongside the diversity of groups. American Indians and blacks have mostly been excluded from this unity, and it is not yet clear on what terms they will be brought in. But political life is in principle open, and this openness has served to diffuse the most radical forms of ethnic competition. The result has not been a weak political order: quite the contrary. Though it has not inspired heated commitment, though politics has not become a mass religion, the republic has been remarkably stable, and state power has grown steadily over time.

Toward Corporatism?

The growth of state power sets the stage for a new kind of pluralist politics. With increasing effect, the state does for all its citizens what the various groups do or try to do for their own adherents. It defends their rights, not only against foreign invasion and domestic violence, but also against persecution, harassment, libel, and discrimination. It celebrates their collective (American) history, establishing national holidays; building monuments, memorials, and museums; supplying educational materials. It acts to sustain their communal life, collecting taxes and providing a host of welfare services. The modern state nationalizes communal activity, and the more energetically it does this, the more taxes it collects, the more services it provides, the harder it becomes for groups to act on their own. State welfare undercuts private philanthropy, much of which was organized within ethnic communities; it makes it harder to sustain private and parochial schools; it erodes the strength of cultural institutions.

All this is justified, and more than justified, by the fact that the various groups were radically unequal in strength and in their ability to provide services for their adherents. Moreover, the social coverage of the ethnic communities was uneven and incomplete. Many Americans never looked for services from any particular group, but turned instead to the state. It is not the case that state officials invaded the spheres of welfare and culture; they were invited in by disadvantaged or hardpressed or assimilated citizens. But now, it is said, pluralism cannot survive unless ethnic groups, as well as individuals, share directly in the benefits of state power. Once again, politics must follow ethnicity, recognizing and supporting communal structures.

What does this mean? First, that the state should defend collective as well as individual rights; second, that the state should expand its official celebrations, to include not only its own history but the history of all the peoples that make up the American people; third, that tax money should be fed into the ethnic communities to help in the financing of bilingual and bicultural education, and of group-oriented welfare services. And if all this is to be done, and fairly done, then it is necessary also that ethnic groups be given, as a matter of right, some sort of representation within the state agencies that do it.

These are far-reaching claims. They have not received, any more than the earlier pluralism did, a clear theoretical statement. They are the stuff of public pronouncements and political agitation. Their full significance is unclear, but the world they point to is a corporatist world, where ethnic groups no longer organize themselves like voluntary associations but have instead some political standing and some legal rights. There is, however, a major difficulty here: groups cannot be assigned rights unless they are first assigned members. There has to be a fixed population with procedures for choosing representatives before there can be representatives acting officially on behalf of that population. But ethnic groups in the United States do not have, and never have had, fixed populations (American Indian tribes are a partial exception). Historically, corporatist arrangements have only been worked out for groups that do. In fact, they have only been worked out when the fixity was guaranteed by a rigid dualism, that is, when two communities were locked into a single state: Flemings and Walloons in Belgium, Greeks and Turks in Cyprus, Christians and Muslims in Lebanon. In such cases, people not identified with one community are virtually certain to be identified with the other. The residual category of intermarried couples and aliens will be small, especially if the two communities are anciently established and territorially based. Problems of identification are likely to arise only in the capital city. (Other sorts of problems arise more generally; these examples hardly invite emulation.)

America's immigrant communities have a radically different character. Each of them has a center of active participants, some of them men and women who have been "born-again," and a much larger periphery of individuals and families who are little more than occasional recipients of services generated at the center. They are communities without boundaries, shading off into a residual mass of people who think of themselves simply as Americans. Borders and border guards are among the first products of a successful national liberation movement, but ethnic assertiveness has no similar outcome. There is no way for the various groups to prevent or regulate individual crossings. Nor can the state do this without the most radical coercion of individuals. It cannot fix the population of the groups unless it forces each citizen to choose an ethnic identity and establishes rigid distinctions among the different identities, of a sort that pluralism by itself has not produced.

It is possible, however, to guarantee representation to ethnic groups without requiring the groups to organize and choose their own spokesmen. The alternative to internal choice is a quota system. Thus, Supreme Court appointments might be constrained by a set of quotas: a certain number of blacks, Jews, Irish and Italian Catholics, and so on, must be serving at any given time. But these men and women would stand in no political relationship to their groups; they would not be responsible agents; nor would they be bound to speak for the interests of their ethnic or religious fellows. They would represent simply by being black (Jewish, Irish) and being *there*, and the Court would be a representative body in the sense that it reflected the pluralism of the larger society in its own membership. It would not matter whether these members came from the center or the periphery of the groups, or whether the groups had clearly defined boundaries, a rich inner life, and so on.

This kind of representation depends only upon external (bureaucratic rather than political) processes, and so it can readily be extended to society at large. Quotas are easy to use in admitting candidates to colleges and professional schools and in hiring them for any sort of employment. Such candidates are not elected but selected, though here, too, there must be a fixed population from which selections can be made. In practice, efforts to identify populations and make quotas possible have been undertaken, with state support, only for oppressed groups. Men and women, marked out as victims or as the children and heirs of victims, have been assigned a right to certain advantages in the selection process; otherwise, it is said, they would not be present at all in schools, professions, and businesses. This is not the place to consider the merits of such a procedure. But it is important to point out that selection by quota functions largely to provide a kind of escape from group life for people whose identity has become a trap. Its chief purpose is to give opportunities to individuals, not a voice to groups. It serves to enhance the wealth of individuals, not necessarily the resources of the ethnic community. The community is strengthened, to be sure, if newly trained men and women return to work among its members, but only a small minority do that. Mostly, they serve, if they serve at all, as role models for other upwardly mobile men and women. When weak and hitherto passive groups mobilize themselves in order to win a place in the quota system, they do so for the sake of that mobility, and are likely to have no further raison d'être once it is achieved.

Considered more generally, there is a certain tension between quota systems and ethnic pluralism, for the administrators of any such system are bound to refuse to recognize differences among the groups. They come by their numbers through simple mathematical calculations. It would be intolerable for them to make judgments as to the character or quality of the different cultures. The tendency of their work, then, is to reproduce within every group to which quotas are applied the same educational and employment patterns. Justice is a function of the identity of the patterns among groups rather than of life chances among individuals. But it is clear that ethnic pluralism by itself would not generate any such identity. Historically specific cultures necessarily produce historically specific patterns of interest and work. This is not to say that pluralism necessarily militates against egalitarian principles, since equality might well take the form (socialists have always expected it to take the form) of roughly equal recompense for different kinds of work. It is not implausible to imagine a heterogeneous but egalitarian society: the heterogeneity, cultural and private; the equality, economic and political. Quotas point, by contrast, toward group uniformity, not individual equality. Though it would be necessary for individuals to identify themselves (or to be identified) as group members in order to receive the benefits of a quota system, these identifications would progressively lose their communal significance. The homogenization of the groups would open the way for the assimilation of their members into a prevailing or evolving national culture.

State and Ethnicity

The state can intervene in two basic ways to structure group life. It can encourage or require the groups to organize themselves in corporatist fashion, assigning a political role to the corporations in the state apparatus. This is the autonomist strategy, the nearest thing to national liberation that is possible under conditions of multiethnicity. The effect of autonomy would be to intensify and institutionalize cultural difference. Alternatively, the state can act to reduce differences among groups by establishing uniform or symmetrical achievement standards for their members. Each group would be represented, though not through any form of collective action, in roughly equal proportions in every area of political, social, and economic life. This is the integrationist strategy: it can be applied in a limited and compensatory way to particular (oppressed) groups or more generally to all groups. Applied generally, its effect would be to repress every sort of cultural specificity, turning ethnic identity into an administrative classification.

What the state cannot do is to reproduce politically the pluralist pattern that the immigrants and their children have spontaneously generated, for that pattern is inherently fluid and indeterminate. Its existence de-

pends upon keeping apart what nation-state and corporatist theory bring together: a state organized coer-
cively to protect rights, a society organized on
voluntarist principles to advance interests (including
cultural and religious interests). State officials provide
a framework within which groups can flourish but
cannot guarantee their flourishing, or even their survival. The only way to provide such guarantees would
be to introduce coercion into the social world, trans-
forming the groups into something like their Old
World originals and denying the whole experience of
immigration, individualism, and communal rebirth.
Nothing like this would appear to be on the American
agenda.

The survival and flourishing of the groups depends
largely upon the vitality of their centers. If that vitality
cannot be sustained, pluralism will prove to be a temporary phenomenon, a way station on the road to
American nationalism. The early pluralists may have
been naïve in their calm assurance that ethnic vitality
would have an enduring life. But they were surely right
to insist that it should not artificially be kept alive, any
more than it should be repressed, by state power. On
the other hand, there is an argument to be made,
against the early pluralists, in favor of providing some
sorts of public support for ethnic activity. It is an argument familiar from economic analysis, having to do
with the character of ethnicity as a collective good.

Individual mobility is the special value but also the
characteristic weakness of American pluralism. It
makes for loose relations between center and periph-

ery; it generates a world without boundaries. In that world, the vitality of the center is tested by its ability to hold on to peripheral men and women and to shape their self-images and their convictions. These men and women, in turn, live off the strength of the center, which they do not have to pay for either in time or money. They are religious and cultural freeloaders, their lives enhanced by a community they do not actively support and by an identity they need not themselves cultivate. There is no way to charge them for what they receive from the center, except when they receive specific sorts of material help. But their most important gain may be nothing more than a certain sense of pride, an aura of ethnicity, otherwise unavailable. Nor is there anything unjust in their freeloading. The people at the center are not being exploited; they want to hold the periphery. Freeloading of this sort is probably inevitable in a free society.

But so long as it exists—that is, so long as ethnicity is experienced as a collective good by large numbers of people—it probably makes sense to permit collective money, taxpayers' money, to seep though the state/ethnic group (state/church) barrier. This is especially important when taxes constitute a significant portion of the national wealth and when the state has undertaken, on behalf of all its citizens, to organize education and welfare. It can be done in a variety of ways, through tax exemptions and rebates, subsidies, matching grants, certificate plans, and so on. The precise mechanisms do not matter, once it is understood that they must stop short of a corporatist system, requiring no particular form of ethnic organization and no administrative classification of members. A rough fairness in the distribution of funds is probably ensured by the normal workings of democratic politics in a heterogeneous society. Ticket-balancing and coalition-building will provide ethnic groups with a kind of informal representation in the allocative process. Democratic politics can be remarkably accommodating to groups, so long as it has to deal only with individuals: voters, candidates, welfare recipients, taxpayers, criminals, all without official ethnic tags. And the accommodation need not be bitterly divisive, though it is sure to generate conflict. Ethnic citizens can be remarkably loyal to a state that protects and fosters private communal life, if that is seen to be equitably done.

The question still remains whether this kind of equity, adapted to the needs of immigrant communities, can successfully be extended to the racial minorities now asserting their own group claims. Racism is the great barrier to a fully developed pluralism and as long as it exists American Indians and blacks, and perhaps Mexican Americans as well, will be tempted by (and torn between) the anti-pluralist alternatives of corporate division and state-sponsored unification. It would be presumptuous to insist that these options are foolish or unwarranted so long as opportunities for group organization and cultural expression are not equally available to all Americans. A state committed to pluralism, however, cannot do anything more than see to it that those opportunities are *available*, not that they are used, and it can only do that by ensuring that all citizens, without reference to their groups, share equally, or roughly equally, in the resources of American life.

Beyond that, distributive justice among groups is bound to be relative to the vitality of their centers and of their committed members. Short of corporatism, the state cannot help groups unable or unwilling to help themselves. It cannot save them from ultimate Americanization. Indeed, it works so as to permit individual escape (assimilation and intermarriage) as well as collective commitment. The primary function of the state, and of politics generally, is to do justice to individuals, and in a pluralist society ethnicity is simply one of the background conditions of this effort. Ethnic identification gives meaning to the lives of many men and women, but it has nothing to do with their standing as citizens. This distinction seems worth defending, even if it makes for a world in which there are no guarantees of meaning. In a culturally homogeneous society the government can foster a particular identity, deliberately merging culture and politics. This the U.S. government cannot do. Pluralism is thus still an experiment, still to be tested against the long-term historical and theoretical power of the nation-state.

2

VOTING
AND PARTIES

Because the United States has always been a highly diverse, pluralistic society, differences among ethnic groups have shaped much of the pattern of American political history. Voters often make political choices as part of such a group, choosing candidates who favor their group and opposing those who threaten it. Groups tend to make the same kinds of choices in one election after another; thus, group patterns form the basis of political party loyalty. Traditionally, economic class and geographic section have been considered the major factors in establishing group voting patterns; but in the last 25 years, however, historians and political scientists have begun to realize that issues arising out of ethnic, cultural, and religious values can be just as real to voters as matters based on class or section.

Voting Patterns

From the 1820s and 1830s, when universal white male suffrage was established in the United States, until the Great Depression a century later, ethnic and religious differences tended to be the most important determinants of political party loyalties. Mass immigration throughout this century accentuated as well as exacerbated differences among groups; widespread suffrage gave free play to the intense emotions aroused. After the cessation of mass immigration in the 1920s, ethnic and religious differences played a diminished but still substantial role in politics. From the beginning of mass suffrage in the 1820s, ethnic groups in the United States diverged in their attitudes toward such culturally explosive issues as prohibition, sabbath observance, public schooling, immigration, slavery, and women suffrage. These issues tended to sort out groups along a political spectrum. Whether a group was pietist or dogmatist in religion, for instance, seems to have made a difference in its political stance. Pietism is a religious impulse in Protestantism that rejects formalism, elaborate ritual, and intellectualism in theology and stresses the techniques of revivalism. The religious opposites of the pietists, in both the Protestant and the Catholic traditions, emphasize formal theology, dogma, and ritual. Pietists insist upon right behavior; dogmatists right belief. In politics, the more pietistic and revivalistic a religious group, the more likely it was to vote Whig (before 1854) or Republican (since 1854). Conversely, the more dogmatic and ritualistic the religious group, the more likely it was to vote Democratic. This pietist-dogmatist dichotomy, however, fails to explain why such highly pietistic groups as Southern Methodists and Southern Baptists have been strong Democrats since the 1850s.

A slightly different interpretation is based on an insider-outsider dichotomy. The closer an ethnoreligious group was to the Yankee Protestant mainstream—that is, the more "inside" it was in cultural terms—the more likely it was to vote Whig or Republican. The more alienated from the mainstream—the more "outside" a group was—the more likely it would be to vote Democratic. While this criterion helps explain the southern Democrats, who felt like outsiders during and after the Civil War crisis, it, too, admits some glaring exceptions. For example, American blacks have probably been the most oppressed outsiders in society, yet they were among the staunchest of Whig-Republican voters until the New Deal years.

Perhaps the best way to distinguish the ethnic constituencies of the two political parties is to examine each group's cultural expectations of government. Groups desiring a morally activist government, one that would intervene to impose moral standards on society, have traditionally favored the Whigs or Republicans. Groups indifferent to or threatened by a morally active government, who instead favored a laissez-faire or hands-off attitude on cultural issues, supported the Democrats. Pietist Yankee insiders therefore upheld the Whig-Republican tradition in order to advance prohibitionist, sabbatarian ideas; blacks supported the same tradition in hopes of a morally activist position on slavery and black rights. Catholics, Lutherans, and other dogmatists supported the Democrats in order to ensure a hands-off attitude on religious issues; so, too, did white Southern pietists to ensure a hands-off attitude on racial issues. A sample political spectrum of selected 19th-century groups might read as follows:

Strongly Whig-Republican:
  Blacks
  Scotch-Irish
  Quakers
  Swedish Lutherans
Moderately Whig-Republican:
  Yankees
  English
  British Canadians
  German sectarians
Moderately Democratic:
  Dutch Reformed
  German Lutheran
  German Reformed
Strongly Democratic:
  French Canadians
  German Catholics
  Irish Catholics
  Southern whites

These ethnocultural attitudes and the political loyalties they engendered remained fairly stable throughout the 19th century and at least until the Great Depression and the New Deal of the 1930s. Andrew Jackson and his followers were recognized as the secular party, the party of live-and-let-live attitudes. Jacksonian Democrats dodged and compromised on the slavery issue, they opposed local prohibition laws, they ran the federal mail trains on Sunday, they proposed no changes in the policy of unrestricted immigration, and in some states they favored voting rights for noncitizens. The Whigs were the Protestant party. Their members not only advocated moral reform causes, but they were constantly tempted by third-party and secret-society enthusiasms. In the 1840s both the antislavery Liberty party and the various native-American parties that made up the Know-Nothing movement, which was antagonistic to immigrants and Catholics, drew supporters from the Whigs.

In the 1850s three powerful cultural movements converged and reshaped the party system. A strong temperance movement took the 1851 Maine prohibition law as a model; the Know-Nothings gained strength as nativist organizations called for restrictions on the Irish and German Catholic immigrants flooding in at mid-century; and the passage of the Kansas-Nebraska Act in 1854 reopened the issue of slavery in the territories, aggravating the sectional hostility between North and South that ultimately resulted in the Civil War. These enthusiasms—temperance, nativism, and anti-Southernism—drew voters away from the Whigs into newer, fresher organizations of reform. Between 1852 and 1856 innumerable coalitions of enthusiasts fielded local political tickets under many different names—Independents, Fusionists, Americans, then finally Republicans. The new morally activist Republican party that emerged in the late 1850s retained the old Whig constituency but with some new additions and a heightened enthusiasm. The Democratic targets of these moral reformers meanwhile huddled together in their reduced but intact political haven.

After the Civil War, politics remained culturally charged. Republicans "waved the bloody shirt" at the former secessionist Democrats; they cooperated with prohibitionists at the local level. In the late 1880s, a series of school controversies energized the Democrats' constituency. The Wisconsin and Illinois legislatures passed laws requiring the use of English in all schools, public and parochial, in their states. These and similar laws in other states threatened the German parochial schools, both Lutheran and Catholic, and enraged most Catholic voters. In 1890 and 1892 the Democrats rode these cultural issues to a string of local, state, and national victories.

Their resurgence, however, was short-lived. The depression of 1893 turned attention from cultural to economic issues, and the Republicans came to power nationwide in 1896. From that year until the Great Depression of the 1930s, the Republicans remained the normal majority party. During this period, the basic ethnic constituencies of each party stayed much the same but the pattern was less clear-cut than in the 19th century. Republican prosperity attracted many normally Democratic voters, and in addition, the Republicans toned down their moralistic appeals. William McKinley, Theodore Roosevelt, and William Howard Taft avoided abrasive cultural issues and made strong ethnic appeals to Catholics. In these years William Jennings Bryan and Woodrow Wilson, as candidates for the Democrats, were identified with pietist, moralist, nativist traditions by many voters; Wilson's election in 1912 was largely a result of Theodore Roosevelt's third-party candidacy drawing support from the Republicans. Though there was no fundamental party realignment in the early 20th century, the Democrats were weaker and lost some of their traditional appeal.

Despite the stability of ethnic political loyalties in the century from 1830 to 1930, party allegiances were not cast in concrete. Some ethnic groups changed their loyalties over time. For example, the pietistic Dutch Reformed immigrants who settled in western Michigan and in Iowa in the late 1840s and the 1850s left the Netherlands in part because they felt the established church in that country had sunk into apathy and lukewarmness. Whig politicians viewed the Dutch newcomers as prime candidates for the moral activism of their party. The Dutch, however, felt insecure and threatened in their new land; they disliked the nativist attitudes of some Whigs and feared (however incorrectly) that Whig activism might lead to a state religion. Thus, the Dutch at first held aloof from American pietists; in the 1850s in both Michigan and Iowa they voted solidly for the Democratic party and its cultural laissez-faire policy. Thirty years later, the Dutch in the Midwest had prospered and no longer felt alien and threatened. Their Protestant pietism and new-found confidence turned Dutch political allegiance to the Republicans from the 1880s onward.

The intensity of ethnic feeling in politics also varied with time and place. Hostile feelings toward a rival group produce the most intense political reactions; and where such negative attitudes are absent, the ethnic factor seems relatively weak. For instance, before the Civil War, the South was the most ethnically homogeneous section of the nation. Though there was religious diversity in the South, there was little hostility among the various groups. A vigorous two-party system existed in most Southern states from 1838 to 1852, but the cleavages were not based primarily on ethnic differences. Whigs were distinguished from Democrats by economic differences, by regional loyalties within states, and by personal loyalties to the party heroes, Henry Clay and Andrew Jackson. After the reopening of the sectional controversy in 1854, however, the two-party system withered in the South. Northern abolitionists were perceived as dangerous to the Southern way of life, and white Southerners increasingly saw themselves as a threatened regional group. Accordingly, they closed ranks behind the champions of threatened groups, the Democrats. After the Civil War and the brief interlude of Reconstruction when Northern troops protected black and other Republican voters, white Southern adherence to the Democratic party became nearly universal and remained so until 1952. Thus, after 1854 the South falls fully within the framework of ethnic politics, with white Southerners among the most strongly Democratic of groups and the few blacks allowed to vote choosing the party of Lincoln and liberation (until the 1930s).

Except in the South before 1852 cultural issues like Prohibition, nativism, abolition, and control of the schools were salient and powerful in shaping a core vote for a particular party within each ethnic group. But economic issues, the personalities of the candidates, and a host of other factors could influence a certain percentage of each group in a given election and thus affect the outcome. If a group ordinarily voted 55 percent Democratic because of that party's underlying cultural orientation, but an economic issue such as the protective tariff convinced just 6 percent of the group to switch to the Republicans, a majority of that group's vote would go to the Republicans. Swings of this sort, and even more extreme ones, happened frequently. For example, Polish immigrants in urban areas were among the staunchest of Democratic voters. From 1888 to 1912, the Polish vote in Chicago averaged 61 percent Democratic in presidential elections. But in 1904, when the Democrats nominated the lackluster, conservative judge Alton B. Parker to run against the popular "trust-busting" Teddy Roosevelt, the Polish Democratic percentage fell to 41 percent.

At two points in American history, economic factors so overshadowed the voters' underlying ethnic loyalties that they affected many groups simultaneously and reoriented the political system. In 1894 and 1896 the politics of depression saddled Grover Cleveland and the Democrats with the blame for hard times and sold the Republican William McKinley to the voters as the "advance agent of prosperity." Enough normally Democratic voters were convinced, particularly groups like the German Lutherans and German Reformed who were only moderately Democratic, so that the Republicans became the normal majority party for almost 40 years. Again in the 1930s economic factors overrode cultural loyalties; nearly all underprivileged ethnic groups in America voted for Franklin Roosevelt in 1936, making the Democrats the majority party up to the present.

The Depression of the 1930s and the consequent Roosevelt revolution in politics were such profound experiences for Americans that they substituted an economic consciousness for an ethnic consciousness as the basic substratum of party loyalty. In 1936 even formerly Republican groups like the Swedes and Norwegians voted for Roosevelt. Black voters moved en masse into the Democratic party and remained there strictly on economic grounds, for the New Deal accomplished little in the civil rights field, even failing to pass an anti-lynching law. Since the 1930s whenever the Democrats sense disaster at the polls and wish to energize their constituency, they do not belabor the cultural imperialism of the Republicans as they would have in the 19th century. Instead, they campaign against the ghost of Herbert Hoover. In the 1970 congressional elections, for example, when Richard Nixon and Spiro Agnew were using law-and-order issues in an attempt to create a Republican majority, the Democrats successfully retained control of Congress by conjuring up voter fears of a recession. Branding the Republicans as the party of hard times is the most effective way of reaching the core of Democratic voters.

Long-range changes in society have facilitated this reorientation of the political system toward economic issues. Mass immigration ceased with the passage of

national-quota laws in the 1920s, and ethnic consciousness slowly diminished with the generations since
then. At the same time society has become more secular, and religion has become a less potent political factor. Even in the 1950s, when churchgoing increased
markedly, the religious spirit remained cool. The slogan of the religious "revival" of the 1950s could be
paraphrased: "Go to church this Sunday; any church
will do." This is not the spirit that engenders fundamental religious cleavages in society or politics.

Although their impact has diminished, ethnic and
religious issues have not become irrelevant in modern-
day politics. The switch of black voters to the Democrats was brought about by the Depression, but since
1948 the Democrats have solidified their appeal to
blacks by championing civil-rights measures. Anti-
Communism in the 1950s was a powerful cultural force
that attracted many Catholic Democrats to the Republican voting column. John Kennedy's Catholicism
brought these voters back to the Democrats in 1960, but
alienated many Protestant voters, particularly in the
usually Democratic South. Throughout the turbulent
1960s, the Republicans frequently used fears of militant
blacks and unconventional youth to lure voters away
from the Democrats.

In recent political history economic and ethnocultural issues seem to have reversed roles. Since the 1930s
economic issues have formed the substratum of party
loyalty, while ethnic, religious, and cultural fears have
occasionally created a swing vote and tipped the bal-
ance. On the strength of the New Deal legacy, the Dem-

ocrats have controlled Congress for all but four years since 1940, but foreign policy issues and cultural fears have allowed the Republicans to win and hold the presidency for 16 of those years. In 1952 Eisenhower and the Republicans campaigned successfully on Korea, Communism, and corruption—not one of which was an economic issue. In 1972 President Nixon was reelected by a landslide, in part because the Democratic candidate, George McGovern, was identified with culturally unconventional and radical groups. As recently as 1976, Jimmy Carter's election was jeopardized by Catholic suspicion of a "born-again" Southern Baptist. Though ethnocultural politics is no longer at the base of party allegiances, it still has important effects on electoral outcomes.

Machine Politics

Although ethnicity formed the basis of party politics through much of American history, it was most visible in the realm of big-city boss politics. Since the middle of the 19th century, the majority of immigrants to America settled in the cities, where the representative of a political machine usually introduced them to American politics.

A machine is simply a party organization: the party structure and the men who run it. But it is a particular kind of organization, one based essentially on armies of party workers kept loyal with jobs and favors. These patronage armies distinguish a political machine from a reform organization, whose canvassers are volunteers fired with idealism, or from a nonpartisan government structure without party workers. At the lowest but most fundamental level of the party machine are its cogwheels, the precinct captains, each responsible for a small district of several hundred voters. Supported by steady but undemanding jobs on the public payroll, precinct captains work nearly full time at getting to know the voters of their districts. They attend weddings and wakes, know who needs a job or a favor, and make a thorough canvass at election time persuading the voters, offering assistance, collecting IOUs.

A score or more precincts form a city ward, presided over by the party's ward committeeman or boss. He appoints the precinct captains and provides jobs for them and their constituents. He is the intermediary at city hall who obtains favors for the voters. Above him is the city boss, more a broker among the competing ward bosses than dictator. He and the ward bosses make up the city or county executive committee, which puts together slates of candidates for office and decides on the division of the all-important jobs and favors.

From the mid-19th century until at least the 1930s, almost every major American city was governed by such a machine. Machine dominance resulted from three factors: American cities had weak governmental structures and lacked a strong municipal tradition; in the 19th century they experienced explosive growth and outgrew what government they did have; and, as they grew, they filled up with diverse ethnic groups who formed separate communities and political interests.

In the early years of the republic, cities were few and

small. Their governments were not complicated or very active. The small volume of city business was handled on a part-time basis by a commercial elite who governed out of a sense of noblesse oblige or else to protect their business interests. From the 1830s on, however, the closed municipal corporation began to be battered by democratization and rapid growth. In the age of Jacksonian democracy, most municipal offices were made elective and the executive power of the mayor was strictly limited. Municipal governments were kept weak by the prevailing fear of centralized authority. At the same time, foreign immigration and country-to-city movements swelled the urban population and expanded the need for municipal services. Faced with these challenges, the part-time patrician leaders withdrew from civic politics to be replaced by full-time professional politicians. City politicians built political machines as informal agents of coordination and centralization to supplement the weak, decentralized formal machinery of government. A disciplined party machine could govern a growing, heterogeneous city, at least partially meeting its needs, whereas the weak formal government could not. If every officeholder depended on the party for advancement and every jobholder on the public payroll owed his livelihood to the party, the bosses could effectively exercise executive authority, no matter what the city charter said.

Immigration and ethnic diversity were not, strictly speaking, essential to the growth of political machines. A large, growing population of poor native-born Americans also provided the conditions for boss rule.

Indeed, the Philadelphia Republican machine received much of its support from native rural migrants to the city. But in fact, most big-city machines were usually firmly rooted in a diverse immigrant constituency.

Immigrants and their children had special needs that political machines were well suited to fill. The bosses found jobs for the men, accompanied them to naturalization hearings, distributed food baskets at Christmas and buckets of coal in the winter. They deferred to each ethnic group's customs and attended festivals and holy days. For all its centralization, a machine was government with a human face. A ward boss or a precinct captain provided favors and personally asked for votes. An immigrant from the decaying feudalism of a peasant village found the city machine congenial.

Civic reformers from the displaced commercial elite or from the growing middle classes found it hard to compete with the personal favors of the bosses. Appeals for honesty and businesslike efficiency seemed remote and irrelevant; their welfare aid, when produced at all, was, in John Boyle O'Reilly's words, "the organized charity scrimped and iced, in the name of a cautious, statistical Christ." Jane Addams, founder of Chicago's Hull House, once related that the biggest mistake she and her colleagues from the settlement house ever made was to ask the county authorities to bury an abandoned orphan girl in a pauper's grave. This action offended the moral sentiments of the girl's immigrant community. The local ward boss, Johnny Powers, on the other hand, not only frequented the neighborhood's wakes and funerals but paid the undertaker and sent a carriage if the family were too poor to pay themselves. Not surprisingly, the Hull House group had little success when they ran reform candidates for alderman against Powers's minions.

A political boss stood ready to assist immigrants at every stage of their new life. Timely advice and favors helped the men find jobs and homes for their families. If the immigrants prospered and went into business for themselves, a political friend helped them secure lucrative city contracts. If they failed and found themselves down and out, skid-row bosses like Hinky Dink Kenna and Bathhouse John Coughlin would find a place for them and other unfortunates in a flophouse, give them a free lunch and a beer, and march them to the polls like a dispirited army. Ward politics was a crude, practical form of cradle-to-grave security.

Political machines also provided recognition and advancement for both individuals and ethnic groups. For the Irish, the Poles, or the Italians, whose members usually started on the lowest rung of the occupational ladder, economic opportunity was blocked by the prejudices of the native-born or by the workers' lack of skills. Ambitious sons of immigrants, without economic security or extended education, often found politics or the rackets the only avenues out of manual labor. Sometimes there was little distinction between the two. A sharp-witted lad made friends on the streets, in gangs, and in saloons, and these friends became a political following, a little cell of dependable votes. Offering these deliverable votes to a ward boss, the aspiring politician then devoted years of hard work to the party as a precinct captain. Loyalty and luck could provide him with a career in politics.

Such political success stories had more than individual importance. When a member of a new immigrant group received a political job or was slated for office, the whole group basked in reflected glory. The ethnically balanced ticket was not only a good vote-getting device, but a psychologically sound means of making an ethnic group feel that it belonged in the wider society. Immigrants were outsiders to American institutions. When important political figures addressed their ethnic associations, sometimes haltingly uttering a few words in their own language; when local bosses helped them with jobs and favors; when their own sons entered politics and held jobs at city hall, they began to feel more like insiders. Thus American politics, under the shrewd manipulation of city bosses, served economic and psychological functions for new ethnic groups, bringing them inside the political system.

The Irish

Irish Catholics have been uniquely active and successful in American politics, yet a few cautions are in order lest their political prowess be exaggerated. Not all political bosses were Irish. The first Tammany Hall mayor of New York, Fernando Wood, was an old-stock American; and the notorious Tammany boss, William Marcy Tweed, was the son of Scottish immigrants. The Republican boss of Cincinnati, George B. Cox, was of English ancestry; and William Hale "Big Bill" Thompson of Chicago was a "Mayflower" American. The Irish neither invented the political machine nor did they keep an exclusive hold on it.

The Irish did not step directly off the boats and into power in the city halls of the nation. Though Irish voters and politicians began to enter Tammany Hall in the 1820s and 1830s, they did not dominate it until after Boss Tweed's downfall in 1871, when "Honest John" Kelly became the first Irish Grand Sachem. The first Irish mayor of a large city was elected in Scranton, Pa., in 1878. The voters chose an Irish mayor in New York in 1880, in Boston in 1884, and in Chicago in 1893. As a general rule, it was at least a generation after the mass migration at mid-century that the Irish came to dominate the politics of any city.

Still the Irish have shown an extraordinary flair for machine politics, and once in power they tended to stay there. Irish Tammanyites ruled New York with only occasional interruptions from the 1880s until 1934. Boston's James Michael Curley repeatedly won re-election to a number of offices over a period of 40 years, despite his reputation for squandering public funds. When the Irish belatedly consolidated their hold on the Chicago Democratic machine in the 1930s, they produced a string of mayors—Kelly, Kennelly, Daley—who ruled the city for 40 years.

Irish success in big-city machines is a product both of their old-country heritage and of the circumstances in which they found themselves after immigration. Though the Irish, fleeing headlong from famine and disease in the late 1840s, were among the most disadvantaged and miserable of immigrants economically, they had many advantages for the practice of politics. Their experience in Ireland had made them both familiar with and contemptuous of Anglo-Saxon legal and political institutions. Because oppressive English penal laws, in force in Ireland from the 17th to the 19th centuries, barred Catholics from politics, the professions, and most avenues for legal redress of grievances, Irish peasants came to rely on illegal people's courts and secret enforcement societies for justice. Thus accustomed to viewing the official government as illegitimate, the Irish were prepared to step into extralegal organizations like the political machines of American cities. Furthermore, though oppressed in Ireland, the Irish had experience in political organization. Daniel O'Connell's Catholic Association of the 1820s, aimed at the emancipation of Catholics from the civil disabilities of the penal laws, had initiated the lowliest of Irishmen into the practices of mass political action. With "monster meetings" and grassroots organization in every Irish parish, the Catholic emancipation movement was a first-rate education in the efficacy of political pressure. The Irish arrived in America with a wealth of experience that later immigrants lacked. Gregariousness and clan loyalties further suited them for the personalized politics of the machine.

Yet it is possible to overemphasize the importance of the Old World heritage in explaining Irish political success in the New World. Typically, it was not immigrants fresh from Ireland who entered politics, but rather their American-born children. Much of the explanation lies in the circumstances in which the American-born Irish found themselves. Their parents' early arrival in America and their knowledge of the English language gave Irish Americans a head start and allowed them to get into political organizations from the ground up. Furthermore, their very poverty and lack of economic prospects in America gave them a strong incentive to explore alternative paths of mobility. The police force and the political machine offered opportunities to shrewd, strong, but unskilled sons of Irish immigrants.

A comparison of the Irish with the Germans, who arrived at the same time in America, is instructive. The Germans had a language barrier to overcome, and they lacked political experience in the fragmented German principalities they had left. On the other hand, most German settlers had more skills, larger cash reserves, and better economic prospects than the hapless famine Irish. Also, many Germans settled on farms far from the large cities and thus had neither reason nor opportunity to seek the favors of bosses or take advantage of the career possibilities offered by politics. So it was the Irish, not the Germans, who moved into the growing political machines of the mid-19th century.

Once in power, the Irish remained in control, not so much through innate natural talents as through skillful manipulation of circumstances. Numerous other immigrant groups followed the Irish into the cities around the turn of the century. None of these successor groups had the political experience of the Irish, but most were in need of alternative avenues of mobility and looked to politics for assistance. The Irish machine leaders appealed to new immigrants with the usual jobs and favors; they extended them recognition by slating them on "balanced" tickets, but reserved the most powerful and prestigious positions for themselves. So many jealous and ambitious ethnic groups were jostling for position in early 20th-century machines that the Irish could assume the role of broker and play the groups off against one another. Poles would resent a Czech being slated for ward committeeman, Poles and Czechs both would resent a Jew, and so on; but all the competing new groups would grumblingly acquiesce if an Irishman retained the position as a compromise. In 1910, for instance, the Irish had dwindled to only 15 percent of Manhattan's population, yet 26 of the 35 Democratic district leaders were still Irish. Irish machine bosses were thus able to divide and rule long after the Irish had ceased to be the most numerous ethnic group in a city.

Irish political success has not been limited to big-city wards. By 1920 numerous Irish Catholic representatives sat in Congress and a number of states had elected Irish governors. Senators David I. Walsh of Massachusetts and Thomas J. Walsh of Montana led the way for a growing number of Irishmen in the upper house of Congress. The only two Catholics to run for the presidency, Alfred E. Smith, who was defeated in 1928, and John F. Kennedy, who succeeded in 1960, were of Irish origin.

Irish-American political fortunes have always been closely tied to the Democratic party, and Irish voters have been consistently Democratic since the Jacksonian era. In the 1870s and early 1880s, as Irish nationalism developed strength in both Ireland and the United States, the Republican party made an attempt to win the Irish vote by rhetorically "twisting the lion's tail"— that is, attacking Great Britain. This policy produced a number of Irish Republican leaders and might have borne fruit in the presidential election of 1884 when the popular James G. Blaine was the Republican candidate. However, Republican hopes of capturing the Irish vote were damaged by an indiscreet Protestant minister who attacked the Democrats as the party of "Rum, Romanism, and Rebellion" a few days before the election. Faced with this and other evidence of continued Republican nativism, the Irish remained within the Democratic party. Thereafter, the only major break in Irish Democratic voting loyalty occurred in 1920 when the Irish were outraged by Woodrow Wilson's pro-British diplomacy and his refusal to include Ireland on the list of nations to benefit from self-determination after World War I. In that year, the Irish and many other ethnic groups unhappy with Wilson's treaty-making contributed heavily to Republican Warren G. Harding's landslide election.

The several faces of Irish-American politics are represented by three 20th-century political figures: The Reverend Charles E. Coughlin, the political radio-priest of the 1930s; John F. Kennedy, elected the first Catholic president in 1960; and Eugene McCarthy, former senator from Minnesota and unsuccessful presidential aspirant in 1968.

Father Coughlin, a pastor in Royal Oak, Mich., rose to prominence in the early 1930s through a weekly radio broadcast and a growing organization he called the National Union for Social Justice. Originally a proponent of papal social doctrines and a supporter of Franklin Roosevelt's New Deal, Coughlin became increasingly shrill as the Depression wore on. He broke with Roosevelt in 1935, helped organize a third-party national ticket in 1936, and began broadcasting harangues that blamed hard times on an international Communist Jewish conspiracy. Coughlin's increasingly paranoid broadcasts appealed to the working-class Irish, especially those who had not advanced much beyond the circumstances of the 19th-century immigrations and whose precarious economic state was similar to that of their countrymen in Belfast or Dublin. Irish toughs responded to the radio-priest's anti-Semitic ravings by attacking Jews in New York, Brooklyn, and Chicago.

Coughlin represents a frightening example of the politics of frustration. He provided scapegoats for Irish Americans who had not fulfilled the American dream of success. Senator Joseph McCarthy of Wisconsin appealed to the same instincts in a part of the Irish community with his anti-Communism crusade of the 1950s. This aspect of Irish politics has receded considerably, for the Irish have become since World War II one of the most middle-class of ethnic groups. Still, the violent response to racially motivated school busing in largely Irish South Boston indicates that this abrasive style of Irish politics has not completely disappeared.

Eugene McCarthy represents a variety of Irish politics quite as eccentric as Coughlin's, but in a different direction. McCarthy's cerebral, intellectual style of antiwar politics in the 1960s was deeply rooted in liberal Catholic social thought. The same papal writings from which Father Coughlin extracted quasifascist doctrines provided liberal Catholics from the city parishes and rural monasteries of the upper Midwest with a coherent vision of a just, humane, and peaceful social order. The Benedictine Abbey of St. John's in Minnesota, where McCarthy once studied for the priesthood, was in the vanguard of American Catholic liturgical and social reform. McCarthy entered politics with a coherent ideology and an intellectual style unusual in an Irish politician. His vision and style carried him through ten years as a congressman, two terms in the U.S. Senate, and a brilliant campaign against the Vietnam war in 1968. But his clerical-intellectual politics as often baffled as dazzled his supporters, and he retired from the Senate in 1970 a lonely and disillusioned figure.

Both Coughlin and McCarthy drew upon authentic parts of the Irish heritage in America, but the mainstream of contemporary Irish politics has flowed in the direction taken by John F. Kennedy. Kennedy represented the economically successful, middle-class, post-ethnic Irish. Never more than a lukewarm Catholic in his personal life, Kennedy gave the impression that his religion had no effect whatever on his policy judgments. In a crucial campaign speech to a Protestant ministers' assembly in Houston, Tex., he decisively dissociated himself from clerical or church influences.

Though his religion was inevitably an issue, and he won Catholic votes and lost Protestant ones because of it, Kennedy's political image was that of the Harvard graduate, not the Irish politician. His cool, pragmatic, opportunistic politics, though perhaps owing something to the heritage of practical ward politics, was sophisticated and urbane in a way that transcended ethnicity. The Kennedy mystique was a national, not an ethnic, phenomenon. Now that most Irish Americans are solidly middle-class in both income and status, the Kennedy style points to the future of Irish political experience in the United States.

The Poles

The political history of Poles in the United States has been far different from that of the Irish, even though both groups have consistently supported the Democratic party. The Poles have not experienced much political success. Few have been elected to statewide offices; and only one, Senator Edmund Muskie of Maine, has become a truly national political figure. Though Polish Americans have become mayors in Detroit, Buffalo, and many smaller cities, the nation's largest Polish community, in Chicago, has never elected a Polish mayor.

The timing of Polish immigration is responsible for some of this relative lack of political success. Poles arrived in large numbers only after 1900; their peak year was 1907. Polish immigrants found the Irish well entrenched in city machines. Also, by the early 20th century, American cities had become so large and diverse that no one group could dominate them by force of numbers. In 1870 the Irish had formed roughly one-third of New York City's electorate. The Poles and other latecomers never accounted for such a large proportion of voters, except in very small cities. Unlike the Irish, the Poles lacked any experience with mass political action in the old country.

The political strategy pursued by most Polish-American leaders also limited political gains. Polish immigrants created one of the densest and most complete complexes of ethnic institutions of any group in America. Polish churches, schools, banks, fraternal societies, and cultural clubs made it possible for many Polish Americans to live their entire life in a Polish milieu. Reflecting this reality, Polish leaders played solidarity politics, organizing around in-group concerns and encouraging a bloc vote. Few attempted to build coalitions by pursuing issues of interest to other groups. As a result, they won elections only in their own ethnic enclaves and were rarely successful in city, state, or national elections where Poles were not a majority of the electorate.

Solidarity politics is a natural result of ethnic defensiveness and probably a necessary first step for any group. However, if a group is large and cohesive like the Poles, it may be tempted to retain this strategy too long and may neglect the skills of broker politics necessary for success in a pluralist society. It is not accidental that the first nationally prominent Polish politician came from the largely Yankee state of Maine. Without the bloc votes of a Polish Chicago or Hamtramck behind him, Edmund Muskie was forced to transcend solidarity politics and appeal to non-Polish voters. Most Polish leaders, however, remain today at an earlier stage of ward and district bloc politics.

Czechs, Lithuanians, Greeks, and other immigrants of the early 20th century were similar to the Poles in their Democratic tendencies, though with many local exceptions

The Germans

Polish and Irish Democrats functioned in an essentially urban milieu. The political history of Germans and Scandinavians showed the form that ethnic politics took in rural areas. Many Norwegians, Danes, and Swedes who immigrated in the 19th century settled on the land, and the Germans were about evenly divided between city and countryside. These groups clustered in the rich farmlands of the upper Midwest, from the Dakotas to Wisconsin, and from the Canadian border to the Missouri River. They were able to participate in politics sooner than immigrants in eastern cities; for in the 19th century most states of the Midwest, eager to attract new settlers, allowed aliens to vote once they had stated their intention to become citizens.

The Germans were the largest and most heterogeneous of the European immigrant groups. Church membership, or the lack of it, was the most reliable guide to German political behavior. The secular-minded forty-eighters and other freethinkers who disdained organized religion and united instead in numerous clubs and societies were most inclined to vote Republican. Members of pietist sects also tended to vote Republican, whereas Lutherans and Reformed church members leaned toward the Democrats. German Catholics were staunchly Democratic. These alignments held firm in normal political times, when underlying party loyalties were the main determinants of voting. However, when powerful ethnic issues affecting the Germans were at stake, all subgroups tended to swing one way or the other in a more unified fashion.

There has long been a myth that the German settlers in the Midwest were strong opponents of slavery and that their massed voting strength was decisive in electing Abraham Lincoln in 1860. This legend, however, is based on little more than the statements of a few prominent German Republicans, such as Carl Schurz, who attempted to claim credit for Lincoln's election. In fact the Germans, like most white Northerners, were not in favor of slavery; but neither did they much like blacks. The whole slavery issue was rather remote from the average German settler and did not touch him personally the way Prohibition, nativism, and sabbatarianism did. For the Germans, 1860 was a normal election; and their votes divided in the usual way, probably with a slight majority for the Democrats.

The first important abnormal election for the Germans occurred in 1890. Illinois and Wisconsin had passed laws prohibiting the use of any language but English in the schools. In Nebraska and other midwestern states antiliquor agitation and a resurgent nativism appeared. All of these forces of moralistic Protestantism, centered in the Republican party, threatened the interests of Germans in the Midwest and produced heavy Democratic votes in state elections in 1890 and the presidential election of 1892. Very quickly, however, this newly united German vote switched sides. Economic depression in 1893 and Democratic fusion with agrarian radicals of the Populist party frightened many Germans; in 1896 the German vote in the presidential election moved over into the Republican column and helped elect William McKinley. With the waning of Populism and the return of prosperity in the late 1890s, German voting returned to its usual fragmented pattern.

World War I affected the German vote more powerfully than the discontents of the 1890s. The outbreak of war in 1914 and the protracted debate over American entry into the conflict produced a rising tide of superpatriotism and sharp attacks on the loyalties of ethnic groups, particularly those of German Americans. Many Republicans, most notably Theodore Roosevelt, attacked American ethnic groups, but in 1916 the Democratic party took a similar stance. Furthermore, most German Americans saw clearly that President Woodrow Wilson's neutrality policy, in effect if not in intention, aided the British far more than the Germans. Consequently, the German vote in 1916 was far less Democratic than usual. Most Germans voted for the Republican, Charles Evans Hughes, while many backed the Socialist candidate, Allan Benson.

Socialists had long claimed a significant minority of

German support, especially among the secular-minded Germans in the cities. Numerous small socialist groups had been formed in the late 19th century by German political émigrés, some of whom had worked with Karl Marx. After the turn of the century, Victor Berger had built a moderate social-democratic machine in the heavily German city of Milwaukee. More reformers than revolutionaries, the Milwaukee socialists first elected a mayor in 1910 and remained powerful locally for decades. In 1916, the antiwar stance of the Socialist Party of America appealed to German Americans, who desperately wanted to avoid war with their former homeland. The party also served as a neutral haven for German voters repelled by the antiethnic attitudes of the two major parties. In German wards of Milwaukee, St. Louis, and Davenport, Iowa, the Socialist Party of America won more than a third of the votes.

In the 1918 state elections the Germans continued to seek candidates not identified with superpatriotism. They favored a Democrat for governor in Iowa, a Republican in Nebraska, an independent farmer-labor candidate in Minnesota, and Socialist Emil Seidel for governor of Wisconsin. In addition, Milwaukee Germans elected Socialist Victor Berger to Congress, even though he was under indictment for antiwar activities. German politics of revenge continued in succeeding presidential elections. German voters joined the anti-Democratic landslide against the Versailles Treaty in 1920; and in 1924 they favored the third-party candidacy of Robert M. La Follette, mainly because as a senator he had voted against the declaration of war on Germany.

World War I had been traumatic for German Americans, and the ensuing years of Hitler's rise to power in the 1930s were no better. The two world wars tremendously accelerated the assimilation of Germans in America. Cultural symbols were rapidly discarded as German Americans tried to forget the past. German politics, as a visible public activity, virtually ceased with World War I. Nevertheless, underlying voter loyalties persisted. Much of the vaunted midwestern isolationism of the 1930s and 1940s can be explained by German-American votes against involvement in a war against Germany. With the replacement of Germany by Soviet Russia as the United States' enemy, however, the last trace of distinctive German political behavior disappeared.

The Scandinavians

The Scandinavians, though divided into three different national groups, were more united in their political loyalty than the Germans. Mostly yeoman farmers, they were attracted to the party of Lincoln by the Homestead Act. Perhaps more fundamentally, the Scandinavians had strong cultural similarities with the Yankee Republicans. The established Lutheran churches of Scandinavia had been swept by repeated religious revivals in the 19th century, and many pioneer immigrants were pietistic dissenters. Scandinavians nursed a strong dislike for Roman Catholicism, and many of them also favored prohibition. The Volstead Act that put prohibition into effect in 1920 was named for Andrew Volstead, a Norwegian congressman from Minnesota. Scandinavian voters, then, were Republican from their first coming until the early decades of this century. Swedes and Norwegians quickly became officeholders in the northern tier of states where they concentrated. Norwegian-born Knute Nelson was elected the first Scandinavian governor in Minnesota in 1892. James Davidson in Wisconsin in 1906, Peter Norbeck in South Dakota in 1916, and a long string of Swedes and Norwegians in Minnesota followed Nelson into Midwest state capitols.

After 1900, however, some Midwest Scandinavians became active in agrarian, third-party movements, protesting the stranglehold of railroad and grain-elevator interests on the farmer's livelihood. Scandinavian farm communities strongly supported both the Nonpartisan League, which rose to power in North Dakota from 1915 to 1920, and the Farmer-Labor party in Minnesota from the 1920s onward. These allegiances do not belie the basic Republican tendency of the Scandinavians, but rather illustrate an important point about that persuasion. The Whig-Republican tradition embraces an independent, antiparty spirit derived from the early Republic. The Constitution made no mention of political parties, for the founding fathers hoped that parties would never take root. Though parties soon proved necessary, the antiparty sentiment never died and often led to splinter movements and third-party action. Whigs and then Republicans preserved this tradition, often scoring the Democrats as "slaves of party."

Thus the independent spirit of politics in heavily Scandinavian Minnesota is part of the Republican tradition. The Farmer-Laborites made a strong protest showing in the 1920s and then came to power in the state from 1931 to 1939. Yet even though Farmer-Labor leaders and voters strongly supported Franklin Roosevelt in national elections, Farmer-Labor did not formally fuse with the Democrats until 1944. Minnesota Democracy was essentially an urban Irish Catholic party; and despite a seemingly natural economic alliance during the Depression, the Scandinavian Farmer-Laborites were reluctant to join with their cultural opposites.

When prosperity returned after World War II, many Scandinavian voters went back to Republican ranks, and much of the moralistic Republican spirit remains. Luther W. Youngdahl, Republican governor of Minnesota in the late 1940s, has been aptly called by his biographer "A Christian in politics." A devout Swedish Lutheran, he attacked the liquor interests, cracked down on slot machines and other forms of gambling, and championed civil rights for blacks. The social gospel politics that seem so eccentric in an Irish Catholic like Eugene McCarthy are part of a long tradition for a Swede like Youngdahl.

The Jews

The paradigm of ethnic voting behavior presented here, with its dichotomy between Protestant moralism and Catholic defensiveness, applies primarily to Christian ethnic groups but it can be adapted for Jewish voting as well. The tiny Jewish minority in the early Republic remembered well the restrictive laws against non-Christians in the colonial era. Thus, a natural defensiveness plus their gratitude to Jefferson, Madison, and other advocates of religious toleration led them to support the Democratic party up to 1850. The German Jews who began to arrive then, however, were a highly emancipated, secularized, and occasionally radical group. Both in Germany and in America they developed a movement called Reform Judaism, which adopted many Protestant practices like hymn singing, organ music, extended sermons, and worship on Sunday. Reform Judaism was, in many ways, a Jewish version of the Yankees' Congregational church. Confident, assimilated, German Reform Jews tended to vote Republican like their pietist Protestant counterparts, and they remained Republican until the 1930s.

Jews from eastern Europe who flooded into New York, Boston, and Chicago after 1880, were much more orthodox and ritualistic than their German coreligionists. Like Christian groups whose religious practices diverged from the Protestant mainstream, Orthodox Jews tended to feel more comfortable in the Democratic party. Two circumstances, however, produced numerous exceptions to this rule. German-Jewish Republican leadership and the strong diplomatic protests of presidents Theodore Roosevelt and William H. Taft against tsarist atrocities produced Republican majorities among Russian Jews in most presidential elections until 1916. Also, the Socialist party had strong appeal for many Jewish voters. Socialism, with its messianic and humanitarian appeals, was a kind of secularized

Judaism for the working class. Jewish Socialist support was strongest on the Lower East Side of New York, where Morris Hillquit and Meyer London were local heroes; in Chicago, Socialist appeal was not much stronger among Jews than among other working-class groups. In any case, voting for Republican presidents and Socialist candidates in New York made Russian-Jewish Democratic support much less monolithic than that of the Irish and Poles.

The diversity in Jewish voting, however, ended in the 1930s. Franklin Roosevelt's social-welfare liberalism appealed to Russian Jews as more practical and concrete than Socialist theories. German Jews, who were generally more comfortable economically, were at first less drawn to the New Deal. But the candidacies of two Democrats of German-Jewish descent, Herbert Lehman and Henry Horner, for governor of New York and Illinois, respectively, together with the anti-Nazi foreign policy of the Roosevelt administration, brought German-Jewish voters into the Democratic fold by the 1936 election. Victory over Hitler in World War II and the Truman administration's support for the state of Israel in 1948 cemented the loyalty of a large majority of Jews to the Democratic party.

Afro-Americans

Along with the Jews, blacks have been the most solidly Democratic group since 1936, but in many ways the Afro-American political experience has been unique. For one thing, no other large group was systematically prevented from voting for so long. Black slaves enjoyed neither political nor civil rights, and most free blacks were also banned from voting. Before the Civil War only the five New England states and, for a time, New York allowed them the franchise. After Emancipation, despite the Fifteenth Amendment that guaranteed all blacks the right to vote, Southern states used numerous devices, such as poll taxes and all-white Democratic primaries, effectively to disfranchise them. Not until the Voting Rights Act of 1965 were all blacks, North and South, given access to the voting booth.

The Afro-American experience is different also because no other large group has changed so completely and permanently from one party allegiance to another. The few blacks permitted to vote before the Civil War overwhelmingly chose the Whigs as the morally activist, antislavery party. The administration voted into office by the Whigs' successor, the Republican party, fought the Civil War and ended slavery, thereby winning the loyalty of most former slaves. During the brief years of Reconstruction in the South, numerous freedmen served as officeholders in Republican state regimes and as Republican representatives in Congress. During the long years from the end of Reconstruction until the New Deal, blacks remained loyal to the party of Lincoln wherever they were permitted to vote; but this allegiance became increasingly vestigial, for after 1890 the Republicans ceased to take any interest in black rights. When the Depression of the 1930s struck black laborers even more severely than whites, they were ready for a change in loyalty. In the 1936 election the black vote moved en masse into the Democratic column. The Democratic record of economic reform and civil rights legislation has kept it there ever since.

In local politics blacks have pursued a strategy similar to that of the Poles. White racism and black pride combined to produce a politics of solidarity successful only in all-black districts. Since 1960, Gary, Ind.; Newark, N.J.; Cleveland, Ohio; and Detroit, Mich., have elected black mayors, but only after blacks became a majority in those cities. Few black politicians have been able to appeal to a broad range of ethnic groups, although Thomas Bradley's election as mayor of largely white Los Angeles provides an exception.

Italians and Others

The Italians, too, as a Catholic group with considerable cultural differences from American society, tended to be most comfortable with the Democrats. However, as in the case of the Jews, several circumstances created an important minority pattern of Republican voting. The small but reasonably confident and prosperous group of Northern Italians who emigrated in the 19th century gave their support to the Republican party in national elections, which often influenced the mass of Southern Italian immigrants who arrived later. Also, the Southern Italian *contadini* were restless peasants with a long tradition of seasonal migration in search of a better living. Once in the United States, they were more mobile, more geographically dispersed, and more opportunistic in pursuit of economic advancement than other contemporary immigrants. If an Italian immigrant prospered in contracting or some other business and saw an advantage in Republican party loyalties, he might well seize the opportunity. Though the majority of Italian voters have probably been Democratic adherents, some well-known Italian politicians, such as former governor of Massachusetts, John Volpe, have been Republicans.

The pattern of systematic discrimination, practiced so long against blacks, has been experienced by other nonwhite groups as well. The federal naturalization act of 1790 prevented nonwhite immigrants from becoming American citizens, and this color bar to citizenship and thus the franchise was not lifted for the Chinese until 1943 and for the Japanese and other nonwhites until 1952. The most recent Hispanic immigrants have probably tended toward the Democrats for both economic and religious reasons, but they present a new pattern in their low rates of voter participation. Though most immigrants have traditionally taken a long time to enter the political system fully, the Spanish-speaking have had distinctive reasons for nonparticipation. Innumerable Mexican immigrants have entered the United States illegally and thus keep a low profile; many others who are legal residents are migrant agricultural laborers who have difficulty establishing a voting residence. Puerto Ricans, though U.S. citizens by birth, frequently remain transients, moving back and forth between their island homeland and the U.S. mainland.

Sometimes a member of a small ethnic group seems to enjoy an advantage over politicians from a large, cohesive group like the blacks or the Poles. The Bohemian-born Anton Cermak, for example, did not fall prey to the temptations of solidarity politics as so many Polish ward bosses did. When Cermak was growing up in Chicago in the early 20th century, the Czechs were not numerous enough to attain much political influence on their own. Cermak, therefore, made himself a multiethnic spokesman on issues like Prohibition, forged important ties with many groups in Chicago, and was elected mayor of the city in 1931.

Occasionally, also, a politician from a tiny minority can serve as a neutral compromise candidate when large blocs disagree. For example, when Mayor Richard J. Daley of Chicago died in 1976, Poles and blacks formed the two largest components of the Democratic party in the city, but neither group would support a member of the other to succeed Daley. The compromise choice was Michael Bilandic, a Croat.

Throughout the history of American politics, one finds both change and continuity in ethnic allegiances. The blacks have switched party loyalties completely, the Swedes and Norwegians changed parties temporarily during the Great Depression, still others such as the Germans and the Jews have varied their political responses. Each group, too, has always had a number of nonaligned, independent voters. Nevertheless, basic group loyalties have been remarkably persistent over time. Group voting patterns often take on a life of their own and persist after the conditions that created them no longer exist. The New Deal party system was based on the economic consciousness of working-class groups. It would seem reasonable to expect that when the Irish, Poles, Italians, and Russian Jews entered the middle class and moved to the suburbs, they would shed their New Deal mentality and switch over to the Republicans. For the most part, this has not happened. Democratic voting has become a group heritage and a reflexive response for these ethnic groups, just as Republican voting was for blacks before the trauma of the Depression broke their loyalty. Both economic and ethnocultural issues make the present group patterns of politics very durable.

3

LEADERSHIP

Leaders may be defined as individuals who exercise decisive influence over others within a context of obligation or common interest. Working from such a broad definition, one can postulate that leadership, like power and authority, is a universal dimension of human society. All peoples arrange themselves into leaders and followers. Yet the importance of leadership varies enormously across the many cultures of mankind. At one end of the scale are tribes without chiefs or even councils of elders. At the other end are despotisms. In the United States leadership has tended toward the more diffuse rather than the more concentrated end of the scale. The high degree of decentralization and specialization in American society have limited the scope of leadership, while popular doubts about the legitimacy of leaders have checked their authority. The same may be said to a greater degree of American ethnic groups. Leaders have been very important at times in the consolidation and maintenance of the nation's ethnic groups, but these groups have rarely recognized any single leader or set of leaders above the local level. Effective central leadership has been a persistent problem for virtually all ethnic groups.

The essential obstacle has been the amorphous character of American society. In its larger configurations—its classes, political parties, and ethnic groups—the society does not reveal cohesive structures. Ethnic groups, with the exception of Indian tribes, lack either a legal definition or a distinct, assured territorial base. Unlike families, cities, or universities, ethnic groups have no encompassing institutional framework through which leaders can control and direct the entire body. The problem may not be acute in particular local settings, where ethnic leaders can frequently develop a stable base. When they reach out to a wider constituency, however, they must contend with the pervasive mobility and the shifting, multiple allegiances that characterize American life.

If an amorphous social structure has tended to weaken and fragment ethnic leadership, it has also given ethnic leaders a special importance. To them in large measure falls the ever-pressing task of defining the group. With certain exceptions, ethnic communities in the United States cannot take their existence for granted, so leaders must clarify what the social structure leaves indistinct or indeterminate. Leaders focus the consciousness of an ethnic group and in doing so make its identity visible.

To highlight the various ways in which ethnic leaders have coped with a fluid society, it is useful to classify them topologically, in the tradition of Kurt Lewin, by looking at the leader's location in relation both to his ethnic community and to the world outside of that community. From this point of view there are three basic situations: (1) received leadership, or leadership *over* an ethnic group, the leader deriving from preceding structures of authority a traditional claim upon the group; (2) internal leadership, or leadership that arises *within* the group and remains there, the leader being rooted in his ethnic group and addressing the external world as its representative and advocate; and (3) projective leadership, or leadership *from* an ethnic group, whereby an individual acquires a following outside of the group with which he or she is identified and thus affects its reputation without being directly subject to its control.

These different situations only begin to suggest the strains, conflicts, and opportunities that challenge those who aspire to leadership. A full account of ethnic leadership would also have to examine carefully the special limitations that massive discrimination has placed on the choices of the leaders of some groups. My emphasis is on tendencies that are generic to ethnic leadership and therefore can be found in varying degrees in groups that have not experienced severe disadvantage as well as those that have.

Received Leadership

Many American ethnic communities have been subject in some degree to received leadership during their formative years. Whenever a new ethnic community comes into being under the domination of an existing institution, at least some of the key leaders derive their authority from that institution and work primarily to realize its ends. Received leaders often failed at the outset to maintain control, but in rare instances their hegemony endured for generations.

In the colonial period many immigrants came to America in organized groups led by persons who sought a new field for exercising an authority grounded in the Old World. The tacksmen who brought large bodies of Scottish Highlanders to America in the middle decades of the 18th century provide a notable example. Tacksmen were leaseholders who collected rents and served as lieutenants for the Highland lairds. When the period of private warfare ended in Scotland and rents escalated, some of the tacksmen induced their tenants to follow them to America, hoping to reconstitute the old clan system in the New World, with themselves as chiefs. The hour was too late for that, but former tacksmen with substantial land grants were important in parts of North Carolina and New York as landlords, justices of the peace, and militia captains and in the American Revolution led their obedient followers to fight for the king.

Of the foreign entrepreneurs who brought immigrants to the United States in the 19th century, the most powerfully entrenched were the Chinese merchant-creditors who ruled San Fraiicisco's Chinatown for many decades. Extending a form of organization that had worked well in Southeast Asia, these merchants formed companies or district associations that found jobs for arriving immigrants; from the immigrants' earnings, the merchants eventually repaid the bankers at the Chinese ports who had advanced the passage money. The district associations gained most of their members from specific regions of South China. Each association served as a benevolent society—caring for the sick, sheltering transients, and arbitrating disputes —as well as an employment agency and an all-powerful creditor. Gradually the associations federated into an umbrella organization that was popularly known after 1862 as the Six Chinese Companies. The headmen of the Six Companies constituted an informal government, whose authority was tacitly acknowledged by civic officials. Thus, in the Chinese-American community a merchant elite acquired a social supremacy that in China itself was reserved for the landed gentry and scholar-officials.

The patterns of leadership that Scottish clansmen and Chinese merchant-creditors transplanted to America were essentially secular. Much more commonly, received leadership was religious, since the traditional institution to which most immigrants felt the deepest loyalty was their church or synagogue. Relatively few immigrants traveled under the direct guidance of a pastor and settled under his care, as did the founders of Germantown, Pa., in 1683 and the Dutch who followed their ministers to Michigan in the 1840s. Over and over again, however, people who came to the United States on their own, in search of economic opportunity, appealed for spiritual leadership to the churches they had left, as soon as they found a new home.

Early settlers necessarily relied on makeshift arrangements for their religious needs. Meeting in saloons or private homes, those who shared a common language and religion resorted to lay preachers or itinerant evangelists, or they joined an established congregation of a more or less related persuasion—but only until a properly qualified pastor arrived from their own country. Some traditional religious leaders gained an unquestioning obedience. The German pastors of the Lutheran Church's Missouri Synod, for example, acquired by the end of the 19th century the paternal authority of the proverbial shepherd over his flock. Often, however, the immigrants proved to be exceedingly indocile charges of the European clergy they had yearned to receive. A spirit of independence, nourished by the circumstances of immigrant life, made for widespread resistance to clerical efforts to impose an Old World discipline. Throughout the 19th century, Catholic laymen of various ethnic antecedents struggled to wrest financial control of their parishes from their priests and bishops. One outcome was the formation in the 1890s of the schismatic Polish National Catholic Church.

Another form of received leadership, quite rare but interesting as an extreme case, was exercised by foreign governments. For a decade before World War I, the prime minister of Hungary supervised a secret program called American Action, which operated through the Hungarian churches in the United States, Catholic and Protestant alike. By influencing ecclesiastical appointments and by subsidizing ethnic schools and newspapers, American Action sought to persuade

Hungarians to retain their Hungarian citizenship and to return to their homeland. In contrast to the secrecy of the Hungarian program, the government of Japan during the same period maintained through its consuls in the United States an open control over the first generation of Japanese Americans. In this case the motive was not so much to retain the allegiance of the immigrants as to protect their reputation and status in a country that had declared them ineligible for citizenship. Accordingly, the Japanese consulate general in San Francisco in 1909 organized the Japanese Association of America, to which all resident Japanese were supposed to belong. The association disciplined the immigrants by controlling their access to certain needed documents; it defended their property rights in American courts and ensured that the leadership of the ethnic community was acquiescent and conformist.

Thus a traditionalist foreign leadership, through economic, religious, or even political connections with the homeland, sometimes imposed itself on an emergent ethnic group. Alternatively, the group might fall under the sway of established American leaders through institutions designed to secure the group's compliance. The Indian reservations, run by government agents and Christian missionaries, are one example, as are the Negro colleges and training institutes that Yankee teachers and missionaries established through the South. Of all the institutions that imposed an external leadership on an American ethnic group, surely the most coercive was plantation slavery. For 200 years white masters wielded over black slaves a control that was both absolute and in some degree paternalistic: so absolute that the slaves could rarely challenge it openly and sufficiently paternalistic (or familylike) that many in both races accepted white leadership of blacks as the natural order.

A primary concern of the external leader was acculturation, because his relation to the ethnic group was precarious and could easily be damaged by a shift in its loyalties. He had to either resist acculturation or control it. The Americans who sought to lead an ethnic community were typically on the side of controlled acculturation. In various ways and degrees, slave owners, Indian agents, missionaries, and white teachers infused into the subordinate group selected habits and values that the host society esteemed. On the other hand, received leaders who operated from bases of authority in Europe or Asia were likely to resist acculturation outright. Fearing that Americanization would undermine religion, family values, and morality, Old World leaders reinforced and perpetuated the immigrants' traditional loyalties.

A received leadership necessarily prevailed whenever the members of an ethnic group were not free to choose their own spokesmen. When that choice existed, received leaders might nonetheless be sustained because of deference, an unquestioning submission to the great ones who had always taken for granted their own right to command. Immigrants from peasant societies often brought such attitudes with them, but habitual deference rarely survived for very long, unless the ethnic group (like the Chinese) was largely cut off from the general American predilection for independence and self-government. Received leadership was usually short-lived and ineffective in ethnic groups that were eligible for American citizenship.

Internal Leadership

No sharp line separates the received leader from a second major type, the internal leader. Although the latter belonged to his ethnic group more completely, the difference was often one of degree. The internal leader might have received his training abroad, as did immigrant journalists who fled from political repression in their homeland and the many Irish priests who flowed from the seminary at Maynooth to the parishes of the New World. His first experience as a leader might have been as the organizer of a mutual-aid society in his native village years before he brought his neighbors together in an identical institution in an American city— a sequence Josef Barton has observed widely among Czechs, Italians, and other southeastern Europeans. The continuities between American ethnic groups and their countries of origin usually permitted an internal leadership to evolve easily and imperceptibly from external initiatives.

Whatever the importance of external initiatives, the task of constituting a self-conscious, self-activating body of people fell mostly on leaders who emerged from and with the unformed group. Not every group, of course, needed to be constituted; the peoples who were already established prior to American occupation

—notably the Hispanic people of the Southwest, the various Indian tribes, and the Hawaiians—lived within a web of relationships that their leaders needed only to preserve, not create. The Indians had their chiefs; Hawaiians their *alii;* Spanish-speaking peasants their *patrónes.* The vast majority of Americans, however, had been torn loose from organic societies and had to produce new leaders in order to forge new ties with one another

Security and Services

Ordinarily the first task of an internal leadership was to provide some minimal security for individuals and families. In an unstable, unfamiliar milieu the newcomers needed the assurance of familiar symbols, the solace of accustomed rituals and promises. Psychological security was best supplied by religion, and that is why religious congregations stand out so vividly as rallying points of ethnic identity. Building churches and synagogues called forth an initiative on the part of laymen that went far beyond what European circumstances permitted. Thus it was not just the clergy who rose to leadership through religion, but also the many parishioners who launched saints' societies, burial societies, sodalities, singing clubs, and so forth. Under the stimulus of American voluntarism as well as of their own need for security, immigrant congregations teemed with associative activity.

In addition to psychological security, the immigrants sought economic security, at least against the most

fearful hazards, illness and death. To that end, even before they built a church, immigrant groups often
formed mutual-benefit societies. Each of these societies, numbering perhaps no more than 20 or 30 people
at the outset, accumulated a mutual insurance fund
from the dues of its members. Often the benefit society
became the nucleus for a religious congregation.
Others affiliated with labor unions or political parties,
but vast numbers functioned as more or less autono-
mous lodges where people from a particular Old World
village could enjoy a continuing sociability. More than
any other institution outside the family, these little societies were the infrastructure of the immigrant world
in the late 19th and early 20th centuries. The profusion
of mutual-benefit societies attests to abundant opportunities for immigrants, many from peasant back-
grounds, to exercise leadership during the decades of
ethnogenesis.

Still another route to leadership was opened by the
immigrants' needs for material services that neither the
church nor the benefit society could satisfy, above all
for help in getting work, but also for travel arrangements, places to stay, familiar food, means of saving
and sending remittances home. To meet those needs,
an ethnic middle class sprang up in the immigrant districts of American cities, consisting of labor recruiters
(known as *padroni* among the Italians), steamship and
travel agents, boarding-house owners, realtors, saloon-
keepers and grocers, immigrant bankers, and notary-
interpreters. Ordinarily a single individual performed
two, three, or more of these functions (he might also be

the president of a mutual-benefit society). Such men were respected as the *prominenti,* the self-made men who had gained prestige and influence among their countrymen by serving as intermediaries with the outside world.

Group Solidarity

One is struck by the multitude of vehicles—the church, the benefit society, the small business—that were available for gaining and exercising influence in the first phase of internal leadership. The diversity of rival mechanisms and aspirants persisted through subsequent phases as well. After the foundation of a local ethnic community was laid, the second major task of the internal leaders was to forge a group-wide solidarity. People who had thought of themselves as belonging to a particular village or province acquired a consciousness of a common national origin. But consolidation failed in almost every case to produce a unified leadership. A single individual has never succeeded in speaking for an entire nationality group; a single organization has rarely if ever gained control of a whole group. Paradoxically, however, the rivalries between competing leaders were a continual stimulus to ethnic nationalism.

The effort to build group-wide solidarity brought into being an array of new organizations. Some of these appealed exclusively to a professional and middle-class elite, while others sought a mass membership. Many of the latter were federations of local benefit societies, often reorganized as fraternal orders with elaborate costumes and rituals. The larger the membership base, the stronger and safer an order's program of benefits was likely to be, and from the 1880s to the 1920s the expanding ethnic fraternal organizations competed keenly for members. Rarely, however, did a single fraternal body gain the preeminence within its own group that B'nai B'rith (f. 1843) won among Jews. In most ethnic groups two or more federations divided the field, the divisions running along religious, political, or class lines.

No less important than the ethnic societies in stimulating group consciousness was the ethnic press; every openly organized element had its organ. The outreach of the ethnic churches, of the federations, of the labor unions, and of the principal political factions depended critically on their newspapers. Even a modest-size group such as the Swedish Americans produced altogether some 1,200 newspapers. The result was a cacophony of voices, in which appeals to group pride mingled with continual denunciations of rival spokesmen for the group. Thus the ethnic journalists had a double effect. On one hand they enlarged the circumference of their readers' loyalties and mobilized mass support for key demands. (One outstanding example was the nationwide campaign launched by Robert Vann's *Pittsburgh Courier* in 1938 for integration of the U.S. armed forces.) On the other hand the endless wrangling between competing editors advertised the divisions within ethnic groups and may have awakened in many readers a skepticism about the claims of all leaders.

Defense of Homeland

The struggle to mobilize a broadly based ethnic consciousness activated the third major task of internal leadership: defense of the homeland. In many if not most American ethnic groups no other issue stirred such passionate feeling, and different perceptions of the problem of the homeland produced especially bitter divisions within groups. Witness the furious conflict between Venizelists and Royalists in the Greek-American community in 1915–1917 and the enmity between Zionists and their opponents among American Jews in the same period. On the other hand, the cause of the homeland could lift an ethnic group to a level of unity that no other issue could. For all groups with a distinctive homeland, this issue presented the critical test of ethnic leadership.

The power of the homeland issue in moving and inspiring an immigrant people was first demonstrated on a large scale by the Irish. Their yearnings for Ireland's independence from Britain shaped the belligerent style and colored the exuberant rhetoric of Irish-American leaders throughout the 19th century. Since 1948 American Jews have taken the place of the Irish as the chief ethnic influence on American foreign policy. Having composed their earlier differences over Zionism, Jews have attained, as champions of Israel, a degree of unity and political power they never enjoyed before.

In recent years an aggressive defense of the homeland has proved highly effective for American Indian tribal leaders, and to a lesser extent it has revitalized the leadership of the Hawaiians. When such a policy runs athwart a national consensus, however, it carries heavy risks. Before U.S. entry into World War I, many German-American spokesmen championed the fatherland with a shrillness that obscured the steady erosion, through assimilation, of the German ethnic community in the United States. Thus the leaders, although unrepresentative, bore some of the responsibility for provoking the extravagant fear of divided loyalties that lashed the entire German-American community in 1917. A wave of anti-German feeling destroyed the principal ethnic federation, the National German-American Alliance, and left any national leadership among the group fatally shattered and discredited.

Group Advancement

A fourth and final task of internal leadership is advancement of the group within the wider society. Like the early concern of internal leaders for establishing a secure base in the United States, group advancement has both a psychological and a material aspect. On the psychological side, advancement has meant a pursuit of status. Here the immediate gains are relatively intangible, having to do with the individual's image of himself and his group. Status goals call for attacking discrimination, widening opportunities, and attaining recognition and visibility. On the material side, group advancement has pointed toward welfare goals: the needs of deprived members of the group for better services and housing, care for the sick and aged, safe streets, and a living wage. The distinction between status goals and welfare goals, proposed by James Q. Wilson to explain the strategies of Negro leaders, may be applied to many other ethnic groups as well.

Status goals appeal especially to the most ambitious and socially mobile elements in an ethnic group. Such people take the lead in forming cultural societies that promote the more dignified aspects of an ethnic group's heritage. It is revealing, for example, that the illustrious Milwaukee Musical Society, which was given an English name in order to attract some Yankee supporters, was founded in 1850 by a recently arrived German merchant, Theodore Wettstein, soon after he had successfully flouted the egalitarian ways of the early German community in Milwaukee by organizing a formal and exclusive ball for the more cultivated of his compatriots. Another type of cultural society that reflects the social aspirations of ethnic elites is the historical association: the American Jewish Historical Society (1892), the American Irish Historical Society (1897), the Association for the Study of Negro Life and History (1915), the American Indian Historical Society (1964), the American Italian Historical Association (1966), to name just a few. Nevertheless, status goals are not necessarily elitist, in spite of their special attraction for elites. While status claims may divide an ethnic group along class lines, they may also unify it if the entire group experiences humiliation. The unparalleled moral authority of Frederick Douglass (c. 1817–1895) in the mid-19th century and of Martin Luther King (1929–1968) a century later flowed from their espousal of a status revolution desired by every technically free black person.

For ethnic groups long dominated by native whites, throwing off the incubus of received leadership has been a crucial status objective. Among blacks even the struggle against slavery left a persisting dependence on whites: on the white philanthropists who dominated the early executive boards of the National Association for the Advancement of Colored People (NAACP, 1910), the National Urban League (1910), and other race-improvement organizations; on the white politicians who gave their black clients access to public offices, on the memory of a white hero like John Brown (1800–1859), who never consulted the blacks he tried to revolutionize. A tendency of blacks to internalize white leadership by choosing their own spokesmen from those with lighter skin suggests how deep the psychology of dependence went. It received one kind of challenge in the 1920s from Marcus Garvey's (1887–1940) flamboyant, ghetto-inspired celebration of blackness and another kind from the light-skinned intellectual W.E.B. DuBois (1868–1963), who advocated racial solidarity for American blacks under their own uncompromised leaders; he broke with the NAACP in 1934 when it refused to alter its course and structure. By the 1970s black leadership (including that of the NAACP) was, in cultural if not in phenotypical terms, effectively black.

Yet the pursuit of better status has required in all ethnic groups something more than a posture of self-respect. It has also required sufficient acculturation to participate in the wider opportunities of American life. Ethnic leaders have had to consider the needs of their people for mastery of the English language, for citizenship and civic activity, for thrifty habits, personal initiative, and suitable economic skills. The tug of these needs often raises a painful dilemma; because acculturation dilutes the ethnic heritage, will it not sooner or later obliterate the ethnic community? Some leaders have thought so and have therefore rejected the goal of success on American terms, instead choosing separate development, exodus, or resistance. Adopted by certain black radicals in times of despair, this position has probably been most strongly and continuously held among American Indians. Ever since white authorities brought great pressure to bear on Indians to adapt to European civilization, the fundamental split among Indian leaders has been between the "friendlies" or "progressives," who accept in some measure the religions and ways of the whites, and the "hostiles" or "traditionalists," who cling to the old ways or try to resurrect them.

Indian traditionalists and the small minority of black nationalists point up by contrast the extent to which the vast majority of ethnic leaders have chosen to compromise on the dilemma of assimilation. Characteristically the internal leaders of American ethnic groups have embraced wider values and applauded American institutions while upholding a limited, nonexclusive ethnic community designed to supplement and enrich the larger society. In general the leaders have served a mediating function, weaving a web of ethnic mutuality on one hand and encouraging their people to reach beyond it on the other. The most stubborn traditionalists are likely to be found in the depressed and isolated depths of an ethnic group, not among its leaders.

The other side of group advancement, analytically distinct from aspirations of status, has to do with welfare needs. In this respect the quasi-assimilationist role of the ethnic leader may not at first stand out so clearly, because most ethnic groups have initially called upon their own resources to relieve the hardships of their neediest countrymen. In the 1840s Bishop John Hughes (1797–1864) built Catholic hospitals and asylums in New York to keep destitute immigrants out of public institutions; about the same time Jews began to create a great complex of welfare facilities. In the long run, the Jewish engagement in welfare has proved exceptional; no other immigrant or minority group has had either the wealth or the ardent philanthropic tradition necessary to manage its own welfare problems, and even the Jews felt overwhelmed by the mass immigration of the late 19th century.

Sooner or later, welfare objectives, like status objectives, have compelled ethnic leaders to turn outward to the larger society to seek accommodations. Whereas gains in status are won on diverse fronts by varied techniques, all welfare claims on the public purse must be negotiated through the medium of politics. The Irish quickly mastered local politics in the United States by a remarkable combination of organizational loyalty, belligerence, and conviviality. Well before the first Irish mayors of New York and Boston were elected in the 1880s, Irish bosses were demonstrating how the political system could yield jobs, food baskets, police protection, and a host of favors. In the 20th century, when welfare programs acquired a more systematic character, ethnic-based politicians like Alfred E. Smith (1873–1944) and Robert F. Wagner (1877–1953) played a large part in passing the legislation.

Yet modern welfare politics also offers an escape from ethnicity. Very few politicians of any stature have so homogeneous a constituency that they can afford to represent just a single group. Through welfare policies that serve broad economic categories, political leaders can generalize their appeal and modulate the clash of competing ethnic interests. Thus the path of welfare politics, perhaps even more than the roads to higher status, draws the ethnic leader toward the margins of his group—and perhaps out of it altogether.

Projective Leadership

Movement out of the ethnic group is, in a still more obvious sense, the underlying thrust of the third type of leadership. Projective leaders are individuals who win their initial recognition outside the limits of the group that nurtured them. In some cases they may feel little identification with that group, but it canonizes them as symbols of its character and submits them as evidence of the group's "contributions" to American civilization. Such leaders are the culture-heroes of American ethnicity. They can ordinarily serve as models for the young because their deeds, while fulfilling conventional expectations, are ascribed in some stereotypical way to their ethnic heritage. Projective leaders repair the self-esteem of groups whose image of themselves has been damaged, and to groups whose culture is fading, projective leaders offer a promise of survival within the mainstream of a multiethnic United States.

Styles in projective leadership have changed. In the 19th and early 20th centuries military heroes, statesmen, businessmen, and inventors loomed large: among the Germans, John Jacob Astor (1763–1848), richest man of his time, and Carl Schurz (1829–1906), Civil War general, U.S. senator, and cabinet official; for the Irish, the consummate diplomat James Cardinal Gibbons (1834–1921) and the "Bonanza King" John Mackay (1831–1902), who parlayed a mining fortune into trans-Atlantic cables and telegraph lines; from the Indians, the peacemakers Pocahontas (1595–1617) and Hiawatha (c. 1570), and the noble warrior Chief Joseph (c. 1840–1904); among Jews, Haym Salomon (c. 1740–1785), who allegedly financed the American Revolution; for southern and eastern Europeans, the electrical inventor Nikola Tesla (1856–1943). For blacks the towering figure was Booker T. Washington (1856–1915), educator and self-made man, who translated the influence he gained among whites into a remarkable career of internal leadership as well.

In recent decades the heroes of war and business have faded, and the idols of sports, the theater, and the arts and sciences have come forward. Nobel Prize-winning physicists such as Albert Einstein (1879–1955) and Enrico Fermi (1901–1954); writers like Saul Bellow (1915–), N. Scott Momaday (1934–), and Alex Haley (1921–); musicians like Duke Ellington (1899–1974); and athletes of many origins have provided a striking proportion of the models of ethnic Americanism in the middle decades of the 20th century.

The Professionalization of Leadership

Whatever the field of activity, however, heroes have shrunk in our time. Neither projective nor internal leaders now possess the charisma that the best of them had in the early 20th century. We have no Cardinal Gibbons, no rabbi whose voice carries like that of Stephen S. Wise (1874–1949), no Martin Luther King, perhaps the last of the charismatic leaders. Counterbalancing the decline of vivid, individual leadership is a growing professionalization and bureaucratization. The rise of professionally trained administrators within the major ethnic organizations is making leadership a more anonymous and collective function, with the leaders becoming submerged in their organizations. At the same time this development seems likely to contribute to the stability and permanence of ethnic groups.

The professional is distinguished not by passion, though he may have that incidentally, but rather by technical competence gained through advanced education. The roots of ethnic professionalism go back to the early years of the 20th century when the National Urban League concerned itself with training black social workers and delivering welfare services in the northern ghettos. The league insisted from the outset that its local affiliates be led by paid professionals.

Professionalization has been carried furthest by American Jews, however. The rabbinate, though confined in its sphere, has been professionalized, and as the great secular apparatus of local Jewish federations, community centers, defense organizations, and educational institutions has expanded, full-time executives supervising staffs of specialists have assumed much of the initiative formerly exercised by wealthy philanthropists. A similar professionalism is spreading through organizations like the National Association of Black Social Workers (f. 1968), the Association of Arab-American University Graduates (f. 1967), and the Italian American Foundation (f. 1976). Notable also are the expanding programs of academic research and publication sponsored by the Polish Institute of Arts and Sciences of America (f. 1942) and the American Hungarian Foundation (f. 1954). More generally, one observes throughout American society the increasing prominence of nonwhites in medicine, law, and public administration.

On the whole, ethnic professionals seem to offer a relatively practical, accommodating style of leadership rather than a highly militant or ideological style. Enjoying widening success and esteem, they are little inclined to jeopardize their improving social status. In general their commitment is to provide effective services while minimizing internal conflict within their groups. In some instances (as among Puerto Ricans and blacks in New York City), a common professionalism has enabled leaders of antagonistic groups to maintain communication and avoid open hostilities. Under the leadership of such "organization men," ethnic groups may be expected more and more to conduct their affairs with the skill and calculation that govern other major interest groups in America. Possibly the distinctions between ethnic groups and other kinds of interest groups may become, in our increasingly professionalized and bureaucratized world, less and less clear.

4

LOYALTIES: DUAL AND DIVIDED

Expatriation is a "natural and inherent right of all people," according to the Act of Congress of July 27, 1868. The specific purpose of the act was to protect the increasing numbers of naturalized Americans whose native countries still made claims on their allegiance, but the choice of language in the declaration was of more general significance. If every person has an inherent right of expatriation, then allegiance to a nation is a matter of individual will. A person may acquire nationality by birth, but as an adult has the right to choose the object of his allegiance. That the Congress should conceive of nationality in these terms is not remarkable; voluntary allegiance is the only possible stance for a nation of immigrants and also for a democracy, but it has not been an easy principle to live with precisely because of these factors.

Immigrant roots have left many Americans with affections and loyalties for the homeland well beyond the immigrant generation; the voluntaristic ethos of the society—its free choice, free movement, free assembly, and free expression of belief—has made it possible for people to express and act on their feelings for the ancestral country. The United States therefore has had to learn to accommodate national loyalties running both to the old country and to the new, a problem especially pressing in the 20th century when greater U.S. involvement in international affairs frequently has forced the issue to the surface of American politics.

The problem took modern shape at the outset of World War I in 1914, when the United States faced the question of whether or not to join England and France in fighting Germany. In debating the interest of the United States in relation to Europe, Americans had to consider what interests they held in common as Americans, what activities, rights, profits, hopes were important enough to the whole society to be worth the lives of young men. This meant that Americans had to confront as well the interests that divided them, particularly the differing interests of the many immigrant groups that had come to the United States during the preceding three decades. Whatever choice the United States made—even the choice of neutrality—inevitably would raise strong feelings among those of its people whose homelands might be jeopardized by its policy.

The World War I experience of divided loyalties within a system of voluntary loyalties raised questions still difficult for Americans to answer. What connections to the homeland are consistent with loyalty to the United States? In what ways is it acceptable for American ethnic groups to express and act on their sympathies for the homeland? In what circumstances? Underlying these questions are more basic ones: what is the nature of the loyalties Americans feel both for the homeland and for the United States, and, perhaps most difficult, how are the requirements of American loyalty established?

Loyalty to the Homeland

Commitment to the interests of the homeland depends on an emotional bond sufficently strong to sustain the considerable time and energy required to express the common concerns of the group. It is a bond that has taken a variety of forms in the experience of American ethnic groups, and that has been expressed with varying degrees of intensity.

Some immigrants in some periods never completely broke ties with the homeland; their primary sense of identity remained rooted in the Old World. This form of attachment was most marked among groups that migrated to the United States without intending to stay, the sojourners who left their native lands usually under economic pressure, to find work, save money, and then return home to resume their former lives.

Many immigrants who came to the United States to seek relief from the depressed state of agriculture in the countries of eastern and southern Europe from the 1880s to 1914—Poles, Italians, Bulgarians, Hungarians, Lithuanians, Romanians, Latvians—came as sojourners and made little effort to put down roots in the United States. Rather, they moved from city to city following the best-paying jobs for unskilled labor and stayed close to other members of their group for comfort and support. Typically they learned little English but concentrated their efforts toward an eventual return to their homeland.

Census figures are inexact, but in the first quarter of the 20th century about a quarter of the Lithuanians who came to the United States, 40 percent of the Poles, and 66 percent of the Hungarians and Romanians returned to their homelands. The Turks had perhaps the highest rate of return in this period: of the 22,000 who immigrated to the United States between 1899 and 1924, 86 percent returned to Turkey. For many immigrants who stayed in the United States the option to leave remained alive and their ties to American habits, institutions, places, and friends remained tentative. Other immigrants, even some who became citizens, expressed their ultimate identification with the homeland by arranging for their bodies to be returned there for burial.

Often the decision to marry in the United States marked the turning point in national identification and created the first tangible tie to the new land. The American-born children of immigrants, far from sustaining a sojourner mentality, often reacted against the foreignness of their parents with an intensity of identification with American culture painful to the older generation.

Immigrants from the bordering countries of Canada and Mexico frequently became commuters without settled national identification in either country. Such ambiguity could be maintained even beyond the first generation because of the ease of access to the ancestral culture and the ease of movement back and forth across the border. This pattern of migration was characteristic of the movement of French Canadians into New York and New England and of Mexicans into the Southwest. The migrants in the United States would return to farms or villages in Mexico or Canada and later remigrate to the United States, where they often formed few connections to the larger society beyond the group. The distinctiveness of the culture and language of these visitor-immigrants perpetuated their separation from other Americans; furthermore, they had less need than other immigrants to bridge this gap, for the proximity of their homelands reinforced their group identities.

Up to the outbreak of World War II, Japanese Americans also succeeded in maintaining cultural identity with the homeland beyond the first immigrant generation. A number of Japanese families in the United States followed the practice of sending at least one child to Japan to be brought up and educated by relatives. These children normally returned to the United States in adolescence and were much more likely to retain the language and customs of the homeland, especially in relation to family, than children educated in American public schools.

Unlike many European sojourners, Japanese Americans who followed this practice usually did not intend to return permanently to Japan but they faced the problem in the United States of general hostility to Asian Americans, expressed, for example, in laws restricting their landholding and eligibility for citizenship. Their bond to the homeland remained strong because legal as well as social barriers kept them from forming normal ties to the new land.

Sometimes the immigrants' unbroken ties with the homeland and their intent to return were of concern not just to themselves but to the country they left behind. The Hungarian government, alarmed at the country's large population loss to the United States at the turn of the century, operated an "American Action" program from 1904 to 1914. The program provided funds for religious and cultural activities in order to retain the loyalty of Hungarian Americans and keep alive their determination to return to the homeland. Administered by Hungarian churches in the United States, both Catholic and Protestant, the program supplied funds to support priests and ministers, to provide down payments on church buildings, to pay teachers and buy books and supplies for Saturday classes in Hungarian language and culture, to subsidize newspapers, even to lobby for health and safety legislation in areas where Hungarians formed a large part of the labor force.

The American Action program explicitly discouraged naturalization and encouraged frequent visits to the homeland, all in aid of a hoped-for repatriation after the immigrants had spent a period of wage-earning in the United States. Although it was successful in keeping the naturalization rate of Hungarians among the lowest of immigrant groups in this period, American Action predictably failed as an effort to retain the hold of the homeland over the second generation.

The government of the new Republic of Turkey, established in 1923, acted even more directly, making grants and loans available to its emigrants abroad to encourage them to return to a homeland badly in need of a work force for development.

For most ethnic groups, certainly for those beyond the first generation, the nature of their feelings for the homeland, their concern about its welfare and interests, were more complex than those of the sojourner-immigrants. Unlike the sojourners, most immigrants and the vast majority of their descendants formed a primary tie to the United States. If they felt loyalty also to the homeland of their parents, it was not because psychologically they had never left it; rather, it was because it represented something important to them despite their having left it—or, in the case of many of the American-born, in spite of their never having seen it.

For a number of American ethnic groups, the sense of connection to the homeland derived from the needs of the group in the United States. For instance, Thomas N. Brown, in *Irish-American Nationalism, 1870–1890* (1966), argues that the essential source of passionate concern for Ireland among Irish Americans in this period was their driving desire for dignity and status in the United States. Poor, despised for their ignorance, their drinking, and their priests, Irish Americans yearned for a source of pride in themselves and sought it in the fight for independence in Ireland. Brown quotes the Irish leader Michael Davitt appealing precisely to these feelings when he promised an Irish-American group in New York in 1880, "Aid us in Ireland to remove the stain of degradation from your birth and the Irish race here in America will get the respect you deserve."

The source of enthusiasm among other ethnic groups for nationalist movements in the homeland also lay in their need for self-respect and for respect from the larger society. There are a number of instances in which nationalist successes in the homeland seem to have stimulated a new interest and enthusiasm for ethnic-group activities. German-American organizations increased greatly in number and size following the unification of Germany in 1870. The success of Mussolini's regime in bringing order and prosperity to Italy in the 1920s evoked an enthusiastic response from Italian Americans who no longer had to rely on past glories as a source of pride in their heritage.

The Zionist mission, the establishment of a Jewish homeland in Palestine, evoked strong though by no means unanimous support among Jewish Americans, who saw in it not only a means for preserving the ancient religion and culture of the Jews, but also a powerful symbol with which to combat the image of weakness, helplessness, dependence on the sufferance of others that had dogged the Jews in the Diaspora. The establishment of the state of Israel in 1948 and its defense against Arab nations in the wars of 1967 and 1973 evoked a tremendous outpouring of emotion and of financial support even among Jewish Americans who were not Zionists.

For other American ethnic groups, nationalist successes in the homeland have produced an ethnic awareness, a sense of ethnic identity and pride, that previously was dormant or repressed. Belgian Americans, for example, who before 1914 considered themselves to be not Belgian but either Flemish or Walloon depending on the part of Belgium they came from, were led by the suffering and heroism of their countrymen in World War I to assume an identity as Belgians and for the first time to designate as Belgian various cultural associations in the United States.

Conversely, immigrants to the United States from the Cape Verde Islands who had always identified themselves as Portuguese Americans responded to the independence of their homeland from Portugal in 1975 by beginning to call themselves Cape Verdeans and by setting up organizations and activities differentiating themselves from Portuguese Americans.

Arab Americans, originally immigrants from Palestine, Egypt, Lebanon, Iraq, Syria, and Jordan, rarely identified themselves as Arabs in the United States until the OPEC nations and the Arab League demonstrated to the world that Arabs were not a peripheral people with an archaic culture, but could exert control over their own affairs, compel the respect of the world, and set their own terms for dealing with it. Coincident with the development of Arab cohesiveness and power in the Middle East has been the growth among Arab Americans of interest and pride in their own ethnicity.

Perhaps most striking is the response among black Americans to the success of movements for national independence in Africa. This has ranged from an enthusiasm for African dress, hairstyles, and names for children, to the politics of militant black nationalism. Like other ethnic groups before them, Afro-Americans have translated renewed pride in their roots to renewed self-respect, confidence, and assertiveness in American society generally. African nationalism has been an important factor in the U.S. civil rights movement and in the development of cohesiveness among black Americans for the promotion of common political and cultural causes.

Loyalty to the United States

The problem for American ethnic groups in balancing and resolving a complex sense of identity is made still more difficult by the complexities surrounding the concept of national loyalty in American political history. The meaning of loyalty to the United States has been complicated from the beginning by the strong tradition of exceptionalism, the tradition of self-perception among Americans based on the conception of the United States as a nation unlike others.

Americans have considered themselves exceptional because their nation is not based as others are on common history, culture, blood, or religion, but on common allegiance to a system designed to accommodate wide differences. It is a system based, in principle, on the liberal ideal of individual freedom—on the right of individuals to follow and promote their own interests, defined by themselves in accordance with their own tastes and values. Because values and interests are the province of the individual, in this system the nation has no proper identity or interest other than the multiple interests of all its people. In the exceptionalist tradition, loyalty to the nation means loyalty to the principle of liberty, and this kind of loyalty is a bond between people and nation that, in the ideal, places no barriers between people of different countries. Americans have considered it superior to the Old World sense of nation, perceived as fostering unity within societies and hostilities among them. Further, the exceptionalist sense of nation leaves open, or even encourages, the possibility of people engaging in activities in other countries according to their own, not the nation's, interest.

Woodrow Wilson articulated this American self-perception, but also touched on a paradox within it, in a speech on May 10, 1915, to a group of newly naturalized citizens in Philadelphia. Addressing the question of national loyalty in terms which must have caused considerable bewilderment, he told his audience, "You have just taken an oath of allegiance to the United States. Of allegiance to whom? Of allegiance to no one unless it be to God . . . You have taken an oath of allegiance to a great ideal, to a great body of principles, to a great hope of the human race." To this instruction he added the "urgent advice" that as U.S. citizens they were "not only . . . to think first of America, but always, also, to think first of humanity." It is impossible, he told them, to love humanity "if you seek to divide humanity into jealous camps."

Implicit in Wilson's remarks, however, is a plea for limitation, for moderation of private demands by American citizens. He was obviously appealing to both new citizens and old not to drag the partisanships of the old country into the politics of the United States. He feared that the passions of Europe brought to the United States could push the nation into war without good cause, and also that the passionate identification of Americans with their European homelands could create divisions threatening social peace at home.

Wilson thus evoked, without examining it directly, a troubling conflict in American belief. The "great ideal" of the United States is to leave people free to express their different interests, but the open expression of dual loyalties inevitably raises problems of conflicting loyalties with the potential for causing trouble both within the United States and between the United States and other countries. Inevitably there has been tension between the principle of allegiance to the ideal of liberty and an American interest in protecting the United States against possible harm from loyalties running to other countries. The problem for Americans during World War I and since has been to try to define the point at which loyalty to the United States makes it unacceptable for ethnic groups to maintain attachments to the homeland or to promote its causes as one of the many types of privately formed interests that Americans are supposedly free to express and support.

Definition of Loyalty: The Law

To a minimal extent, this point is defined by law. Congress passed major nationality laws in 1907, 1940, and 1952 mainly to codify regulations for acquiring citizenship (*see* Naturalization and Citizenship), but these laws also provided for deprivation of citizenship for activities that demonstrated a primary loyalty elsewhere. The first law, in 1907, defined the following grounds for loss of U.S. citizenship: naturalization in another country; taking an oath of allegiance to another country; for naturalized Americans, leaving the United States and living in the native country for two years or in any foreign country for five; and for American women, marrying an alien regardless of where they live thereafter. Loss of citizenship by marriage was repealed partially in 1922 and wholly in 1931, but otherwise the 1907 law was maintained nearly intact in the 1940 and 1952 codifications. The later acts lengthened the amount of time naturalized Americans could live abroad without jeopardizing their U.S. citizenship, but they also specified additional types of behavior as inconsistent with allegiance to the United States.

The 1940 act provided for loss of citizenship for any person fighting in the armed forces of a foreign state if he was also a national of that state. The 1952 act and subsequent amendments dropped the condition of foreign nationality but added the provision that citizenship remain intact if the foreign armed service was authorized by the Secretary of State or Defense, with further protections of citizenship if the person in question was under 18. Under the 1940 law Americans could also lose citizenship if employed by a foreign government in positions for which only nationals were eligible. This provision was revised in the later law to apply only to Americans working for foreign governments who were also nationals of the foreign state or whose jobs required an oath of allegiance to that state. Under both the 1940 and 1952 laws an American was liable to loss of citizenship for voting in a foreign election.

The laws in the statute books (currently United States Code 8, Section 1481: Loss of Nationality) appear to provide one area of clarity, however limited, in the larger question of the meaning of loyalty, but even these apparently straightforward rules have been difficult to apply in practice because of the ever-present influence of the exceptionalist tradition. The exceptionalist emphasis on individual freedom lends strength to demands for freedom to express and act on loyalties to other nations as well as to the United States. This principle, as well as the strong interest of many Americans in maintaining connections to other countries, has been the basis for constant resistance to the limits placed by U.S. nationality laws on the exercise of dual loyalties. As a result of court challenges over the years, the laws at present have much less restrictive force than their wording would suggest.

From the beginning, administrators and courts interpreting nationality law generally followed the principle that conduct in breach of the law called for loss of citizenship only if undertaken knowingly and voluntarily. If confusion or duress were involved, it was assumed that the person was engaging in the proscribed activity not out of attachment to the foreign government, but for other reasons possibly compatible with loyalty to the United States. Judges looked for evidence of an actual, subjective transfer of allegiance to another country. If there was good evidence to the contrary, the loss of citizenship was generally not imposed.

Under this view of the law, passport officers, tax officials, other administrators, and courts had to assess not only the activities of U.S. citizens abroad, but also the state of their hearts and minds. Thus the American who voted in a Romanian election because the penalty for not voting was five years' hard labor did not lose his U.S. citizenship. Nor did the woman who married an alien thinking he was an American citizen and left him as soon as she discovered he was not. Nor ultimately did most of the hundreds of Italian and Japanese Americans who were dual nationals living abroad at the start of World War II and were drafted, without choice, into the Italian and Japanese armies. Many of the men who fought in enemy armies and sought to return to the United States after the war initially were denied passports under the 1940 law because they had served in foreign armies, but subsequent administrative and judicial reviews firmly established the principle that when the service was not voluntary the letter of the law did not apply.

More recently the Supreme Court has invalidated several parts of the law on loss of nationality as unconstitutional abridgments of the rights of citizens and has placed drastic limits on the rest of the law. In 1964 in *Schneider* v. *Rusk,* the Court found unconstitutional the law imposing loss of citizenship on naturalized Americans who lived abroad beyond a certain period because the stipulation did not apply equally to native-born citizens; the Court found it discriminatory to the point of denying due process to naturalized citizens. In *Afroyim* v. *Rusk* (1967) the Court declared that loss of citizenship because of voting in a foreign election was also unconstitutional. The plaintiff Afroyim was an American who had lived in Israel for ten years. When he sought an American passport to return to the United States, the passport was denied on grounds that Afroyim had voted in an Israeli election. In finding it unconstitutional to deprive a person of citizenship for this reason, the Court specifically reversed a 1958 decision (*Perez* v. *Brownell*).

The significance of the *Afroyim* decision goes beyond the issue of voting, however, for in reaching its conclusion the Court enunciated a broad new doctrine concerning the rights of citizenship. Justice Hugo Black, writing for the Court, declared that the Fourteenth Amendment citizenship clause confirmed U.S. citizenship as a right that Congress had no authority to alter. Rather, the amendment gave every citizen "a constitutional right to remain a citizen in a free country unless he voluntarily relinquishes that citizenship." Thus, the Court, acting on the libertarian premises implicit in the tradition of exceptionalism, recognized the individual and not the nation as the ultimate arbiter of his own loyalty.

Since *Afroyim,* the law on loss of nationality has stood as written in 1952, except for deletion of the sections applying to voting in foreign elections and to naturalized citizens living abroad (as well as changes in other sections not relating to dual allegiances), but the force of the law has been radically reduced. According to an attorney general's opinion interpreting *Afroyim* in 1969, loss of citizenship can be imposed for activities still specified in the law only when the U.S. citizen engaging in them *intends* by doing so to relinquish his citizenship. As a practical matter, short of formal renunciation of citizenship American citizens legally have virtually unlimited scope for the expression of dual loyalties.

Definition of Loyalty: Public Opinion

The requirements of loyalty are no longer—if they ever were—clearly defined by law; a more potent force affecting the limits of homeland loyalties has been the pressure of public opinion. The effective line between acceptable and unacceptable connections to the homeland has been drawn largely by popular reaction, incident by incident, to various ways ethnic groups have been involved in affairs of their homelands. Sometimes appeals for the homeland have aroused positive public enthusiasm; at other times, merely tolerance or indifference. Occasionally ethnic groups have faced public hostility and charges of disloyalty for their identification with the homeland.

The reasons for perceptions of disloyalty, when they have occurred, are extremely difficult to isolate. Sometimes there has been genuine fear that ethnic-group activities threatened the interests of the United States. However, such fears have often been mixed with tensions stemming from domestic, not international, conflicts. For an ethnic group to identify with the homeland is to emphasize foreignness, difference, and thus to arouse the always volatile fears and suspicions present in a heterogeneous society. If public opinion is the only effective measure of loyalty and disloyalty in the United States, it is also a measure that indicates the close relation between American conceptions of loyalty and American capacities for tolerance of internal differences. At some points the distinction disappears and accusations of disloyalty are clearly reflections of nothing more than the continuing force of racial and ethnic prejudice.

Private Support for the Homeland

Among the least controversial activities of American ethnic groups has been the use of their own private resources to support causes in the homeland. Such efforts are consistent with the overriding tradition of privatism in American society and have been considered no less legitimate than those of thousands of other groups in the United States that promote causes of their own choosing. The most widely practiced form of direct support for the homeland has been that of raising funds in the United States to aid relatives abroad or more generally for organized charity in periods of special need, but also for political purposes in times of national crisis.

During World War I, eastern European groups in the United States were especially active in support of the war efforts of homeland governments, either through the purchase of their war bonds or through contributions to organizations raising funds in aid of the homeland. The Central Committee of the Serbian National Defense, founded in New York in 1914, raised over a half-million dollars for Serbia during the war; Czechs and Slovaks in the United States contributed $675,000 to the Czechoslovak National Council to finance efforts to win support for the formation of an independent Czechoslovak state after the war. Polish Americans raised a quarter-million dollars in liberty bonds to support the formation of an independent Poland. In the immediate postwar years Lithuanian Americans raised $2,000,000 through the sale of Lithuanian Freedom Loan Bonds to aid the establishment of an independent Lithuanian nation. The largest amounts of money sent from the United States during and after World War I were raised by the American Jewish Joint Distribution Committee to provide relief for the massive numbers of displaced Jews in eastern Europe and Turkey. It contributed over $16.5 million during the war and another $47.5 million from 1918 to 1922 to a network of organizations in Europe.

American ethnic groups whose homeland causes were lost during the war raised substantial amounts of money in the postwar years to help support refugees or impoverished families who remained in the homeland. The Boston-based Education of Russian Youth in Exile sent $300,000 for the education of Russian refugees in various parts of Europe in the 1920s. Carpatho-Rusyns in the United States sent millions of dollars in aid to the homeland from 1918 to 1938 when, having failed to establish its own autonomy, it was under the uneasy jurisdiction of the new state of Czechoslovakia. Ukrainian Americans raised $140,000 in the immediate post-war years for a Ukrainian government in exile and throughout the 1930s sent hundreds of thousands of dollars to support charitable, educational, and political institutions in the homeland.

For many Asian Americans in the same period, the plight of homelands threatened or occupied by Japan elicited continuing concern and financial support. Korean Americans formed various nationalist organizations and raised money throughout the period, from 1910 to 1945, of Japanese colonial rule in Korea. Chinese Americans aided the defense of China against Japan from 1937 to 1945 through the purchase of millions of dollars of Chinese war bonds.

After World War II the outpouring of private relief funds for European countries supplemented official relief and rehabilitation programs funded by the U.S. government and by international organizations. As in World War I, eastern European ethnic groups were especially energetic and successful in sending cash, clothing, food, and supplies to their homelands, although the amounts that could be sent were severely restricted in the countries that fell under the control of the Soviet Union in the late 1940s.

In the period following World War II as in the years after 1918, the single largest fund-raising effort was that of Jewish Americans, this time in support of the state of Israel, which was founded in 1948. After that event about 60 percent of the funds collected annually by federated Jewish philanthropies in the United States went to Israel, except in times of crisis when the percentage was higher. The largest amount raised in any year was the $600 million contributed by Jewish Americans in the aftermath of the 1973 war with Egypt, when the strength of the Egyptian forces had caught Israel off guard and placed it in serious jeopardy.

Army Service

In addition to buying war bonds and sending food, clothing, and medical supplies to relieve the hardships of war, members of American ethnic groups have expressed their continued loyalty most directly by volunteering to fight for the homeland cause. This was particularly the case in World War I before the United States itself became engaged. The Serbian-American community, which had been actively involved in resistance to Austria-Hungary for several years before the war, sent thousands of young men to serve with the Serbian army when war broke out in 1914. Similarly, the Pan-Hellenic Union recruited 42,000 young Greek Americans to fight for Greece in the Balkan wars of 1912 and 1913. Before the United States entered World War I, many Polish Americans fought with European armies in the hope of promoting Polish independence.

Fighting for the homeland became more complicated after the Nationality Act of 1940 made service in a foreign army grounds for loss of citizenship, but the comparatively early entry of the United States into World War II made joining the homeland cause a different issue from that of the earlier war. A number of young men who fought with foreign armies in World War I were liable to loss of citizenship not for joining foreign forces, but for taking the necessary oath of allegiance to the government involved. Congress, however, in a law passed on May 9, 1918, absolved them of this forfeiture if they had fought against a country "with which the United States is now at war."

Engagement in Homeland Politics

In periods of intense political struggle in the homeland, the more politically active elements of American ethnic groups, often recent émigrés, engaged directly in the struggle through involvement with one of the contending factions. Fund-raising was usually an important activity of such groups, but in addition some served as long-distance analysts, advisers, and critics, guiding or even directing the efforts of their counterparts in the homeland. Often, however, the energies of American-based leaders of homeland factions have been consumed in quarrels among themselves.

Irish Americans, before the granting of Irish independence in 1921, had a long history of factional involvement in the Irish resistance to English control. As early as the 1820s Irish associations in the United States supported Daniel O'Connell's fight for Catholic Emancipation and repeal of the Act of Union which made Ireland an integral part of England. In 1857 the Irish Republican Brotherhood (the Fenians) was formed to raise funds for homeland leaders but also to organize and train forces for direct participation in the rising against England which the Fenians advocated and one faction actually attempted in 1867. The Clan na Gael, or United Brotherhood, founded in 1867 on a broader social base than the primarily working-class Fenians, joined with other nationalist groups in the 1880s in support of Charles Stewart Parnell's Home Rule movement. This group in the 1890s turned to several ventures in terrorism both in England and in the United States that divided the movement again.

In 1910, British acceptance of the principle of Home Rule reduced the direct engagement of Irish Americans in the factional politics of Ireland, but fund-raising in the United States for nationalist groups fighting for the elimination of all ties with England remained vigorous until the De Valera constitution of 1937 established the independent state of Eire. Some support from Irish Americans for the Irish Republican Army and for other groups carrying on anti-British activities in Northern Ireland never completely stopped, and increased in the 1960s with the outbreak of fighting between the Catholics and Protestants of Ulster.

In the 1970s influential Irish-American politicians, including House Speaker Thomas P. O'Neill, Jr., Senator Edward M. Kennedy of Massachusetts, and Governor Hugh L. Carey and Senator Daniel Patrick Moynihan of New York, attempted through visits and pronouncements to aid the cause of a united Ireland detached from England, while opposing private American aid for groups using violence in the fight for unity.

During World War I, eastern European and Balkan émigrés in the United States were deeply involved in the issues, choices, and strategies of political factions in the homeland. Croatian Americans formed the Croatian National Alliance in Kansas City in 1912 to organize political action against Hapsburg control and to support the establishment of a South Slav state made up of Croatia, Serbia, and Slovenia. The alliance's program included such terrorist tactics as the attempted assassination of a Hapsburg official in Zagreb in 1913, only a year before the assassination of the Archduke Franz Ferdinand in Serbia precipitated the outbreak of war.

Albanian Americans, most notably the liberal-socialist Bishop Fan Noli, played a key role through the Pan Albanian Federation of America (VATRA) in gaining backing for an independent Albania at the London Conference of 1913, convened to settle the controversies arising out of the Balkan wars. After World War I nullified the arrangements made at this conference, Noli again was instrumental in gaining the support of Woodrow Wilson, who pressed for Albanian independence at Versailles.

Perhaps the most remarkable instance of direct involvement of an American ethnic group in the politics of the homeland was the massive letter-writing campaign by Italian Americans to urge relatives and friends in Italy to vote against Communist candidates in the Italian election of April 1948. The campaign was organized through Catholic churches serving the Italian community. The clergy distributed form letters and urged in Sunday sermons that parishioners advise people in the homeland to vote for the Christian Democratic party because of its support of democracy and the church. In communities where the local church made a strong appeal, about 40 percent of the parishioners sent letters back to Italy. The deluge of letters was large enough to become a campaign issue; Socialists and Communists attacked the letters as interference and dictation in Italian affairs. The Christian Democrats, for whatever reason, won the election overwhelmingly.

Return to the Homeland

Another form of direct support by American ethnic groups for homeland causes—the ultimate possible commitment—is to move to the homeland to live and. work. The most notable experience of return from the United States to the ancestral country has been that of Jewish American Zionists leaving the United States to take up permanent residence and citizenship in Israel.

The American Zionist movement took institutional form in 1915 with the establishment of the American Jewish Congress. It was opposed then and in subsequent years by the generally more conservative American Jewish Committee, whose position was that ethnic bonds among Jews were primarily religious and cultural and did not preclude social and political assimilation into the life of the nations of which Jews had become citizens. This was thought to be especially true of the United States with its openness and commitment to toleration. The Zionist commitment to establishment of a Jewish state in Palestine necessarily lent a secular political dimension to Jewish identity that challenged assimilationist attitudes.

The issue became more intense for the Jewish-American community with the founding of Israel, for the new state desperately needed settlers to work the land, build industries, and maintain defenses. Its need touched the conscience of Jews whether Zionist or not. The conflict of loyalties for Jewish Americans was intensified by the Knesset's passage in 1950 of the Law of Return, which declared all Jews everywhere eligible for Israeli citizenship. Furthermore, the Israeli government attempted to make it as easy as possible for Jewish Americans to become Israeli citizens without losing U.S. citizenship. Its 1952 nationality law was designed purposely to minimize conflict with the U.S. law passed the same year. The Israeli law automatically conferred citizenship on all Jews living in Israel for a specified time without requiring a renunciation of other citizenship or an oath of allegiance to Israel, either of which would have been grounds for loss of U.S. nationality. Under these laws, levels of emigration from the United States to Israel have been steady but not high, rarely more than 500 a year in the 1950s and early 1960s. However, the number mounted to about 6,000 annually in the four years following the 1967 war.

All these private activities of American ethnic groups—whether buying Polish or Chinese war bonds, joining the Greek army, negotiating for the independence of Albania, or living in Israel for a period of years—are expressions of intense commitment to a nation other than the United States, and the intensity of such involvement might well be expected to raise questions of conflict with loyalty to the United States. Instead, such behavior, carried out within the sphere of the private actions of ethnic groups, has become so completely expected and accepted that it has scarcely been a matter of notice other than in time of war.

Homeland Issues in American Elections

When American ethnic groups have moved from the private to the public sphere to organize support for the homeland or otherwise to protect its interests as they are affected by the policies of the U.S. government, they have moved onto less certain ground. Efforts to relate a cause in the homeland to a more general American one necessarily invite negative reactions by other segments of the society, and at least the possibility of attack on its ethnic proponents. Some forms of political activity, however, have proved more generally acceptable than others.

One traditional means for promoting policies favorable to the homeland has been to attempt to make the desired policy an issue for candidates facing an election; this tactic has produced mixed results in terms of affecting policy, but generally has been accepted as a legitimate means of expressing ethnic-group concerns. The first to employ this tactic were the Irish Americans who began to make U.S. relations with Ireland's archenemy, England, a campaign issue as far back as the 1840s, when they attempted to exploit the dispute between Britain and the United States over the Oregon territory. In 1888 the Irish contributed to Benjamin Harrison's defeat of President Grover Cleveland when Republicans used Cleveland's attempts to sign a fisheries agreement with England to label him pro-British. The Republicans also provoked a virtual endorsement of Cleveland by the British Ambassador Sir Lionel Sackville-West on the eve of the election, which further aroused Irish indignation.

In 1897 the Senate rejected an arbitration treaty with England in the wake of heavy Irish lobbying against it. Any inclination of officials at the State Department to offer support to England during the Boer War was effectively discouraged by the combined and vocal opposition of both Irish and German Americans, a formidable constituency carefully courted by both Democratic and Republican candidates for office.

With the advent of World War I in 1914, the consequences of U.S. policy toward Old World countries became far more complex. From this point on, U.S. foreign policy inevitably affected American society generally, and seriously enough so that the demands of a particular ethnic group had to be weighed against the effect of policy on a wide range of groups or on the nation as a whole. The Irish, for example, after the Easter Rising in 1916, tried before the presidential election to gain Wilson's support for protection of the leaders of the rising. Wilson, however, necessarily concerned about the wider issue of British strength against Germany, refused to help in spite of the apparent closeness of the election.

The election of Warren Harding to the presidency in 1920 was aided by the defection of the Irish from the Democratic party because of bitterness over Wilson's failure to demand immediate independence for Ireland, as well as by the temporary defection to the Republicans of other, smaller ethnic groups—Italians, Greeks, Lithuanians, and Chinese, for example—disappointed in postwar U.S. policy toward their homelands.

The memory of the political disaster of 1920 inspired the Democrats, again facing a postwar election in 1948, to use the Nationalities Division of their campaign organization to counteract the potential defection of ethnic groups with grievances about American policies toward the homeland. Polish Americans were disappointed by the lack of effective support for non-Communist forces in Poland, as were Jewish Americans by the uncertain U.S. policy toward Palestine. Italian Americans were courted by Republicans promising to support the reestablishment of Italy's control over its former African colonies.

The Democratic appeal to these groups was cast largely in terms of domestic issues. The heavily Democratic returns from these groups were generally interpreted as crucial to Harry Truman's victory, but also as indicative of the primacy of pocketbook issues over homeland concerns in the voting habits of ethnic groups.

Whether Jewish-American voters, since 1932 predominantly liberal Democrats, would have defected to the Republicans over the issue of Palestine was never tested; Truman's immediate recognition of the state of Israel in May 1948 decisively removed the homeland cause as an election issue. The intriguing, but ultimately unanswerable, question remains whether Truman's act was motivated by the Jewish vote. Truman maintained that domestic politics played no part in his decision, that it was based on his conception of what was right and what was possible with respect to a Jewish homeland.

The raising of homeland issues at election time, both by ethnic groups seeking official attention and by candidates seeking ethnic votes, continues, as do the ritual visits of candidates to the three *Is*—Israel, Italy, and Ireland. However, the gravity of the factors involved in U.S. foreign policy in the years after World War II has substantially reduced both the possibility of official response to ethnic demands as such and the expectation by ethnic groups that such response would be possible.

Lobbying for a Friendly Homeland

Although the kinds of issues raised in election years by ethnic groups have tended to be specific ones of fairly immediate concern for the homeland, a number of groups have also engaged in longer-range public campaigning designed to achieve more basic foreign-policy commitments. During World War I various groups mounted successful lobbying efforts for causes in the homeland. Eastern Europeans whose homelands had been part of the empires collapsing in the war campaigned vigorously for American backing for postwar independence. Heartened by Woodrow Wilson's proclamation of the principle of self-determination, Poles, Czechs, Slovaks, Ukrainians, Lithuanians, Armenians, Albanians, and Croats organized campaigns to convince Wilson to carry support for the homeland cause into the peace negotiations.

Some were more successful than others. The Czechs were at first dismayed by Wilson's announcement in January 1918 of a peace plan that provided some autonomy for ethnic units within Austria-Hungary but not for dissolution of the empire. They protested this plan energetically, and in May 1918 staged mass rallies across the country to bring the issue of Czech independence before the public. Tomas Masaryk, the exiled nationalist leader, traveled from rally to rally addressing the crowds. Wilson met with Masaryk and in September 1918 announced his support for an independent Czech-Slovak state, the position later adopted by the peace conference.

Albanians, Poles, and Croats also gained Wilson's support, as did the cause of an independent Armenia. The U.S. government recognized the Republic of Armenia when it was proclaimed in 1920, but was not willing to reengage in war in Europe to defend it when it was reoccupied by Russia only a few months after its founding, or when it was subsequently divided between Russia and Turkey. The initiative and persistence of the ethnic group in making the homeland cause an issue for the U.S. government contributed to the success of those that won official support, but in no case was a group successful when the promotion of its cause appeared militarily or diplomatically threatening to the United States. Loyalty to the United States requires that at some point ethnic group demands for the homeland must be subordinated to the larger interests of the country; this point has been defined by resistance from American leaders or the public generally to demands that seem too costly to the country as a whole. During World War I, for example, no amount of pressure from Irish Americans, regardless of their importance to the Democratic party, could move President Wilson to demand that the British grant immediate independence to Ireland.

Later, with the reversal suffered in World War II and afterward by most of the eastern European nations that had won their independence only 20 years earlier, American ethnic groups again organized to demand renewed guarantees from the U.S. government for the independence of their homelands, but this time without success. The United States could not contest Soviet control over the governments of eastern Europe without the risk of war. Thus, in response to the pleas of American ethnic groups, the government made rhetorical gestures of protest only when the Soviet Union incorporated the nations of Latvia, Lithuania, and Estonia and imposed subservient Communist governments in Poland, East Germany, Hungary, Czechoslovakia, Romania, Bulgaria, and Albania. At the height of the Cold War in the mid-1950s, the Eisenhower administration stated a commitment in principle to the liberation of these nations—to "liberating enslaved peoples," the president said. In practical terms, however, U.S. postwar policy in Europe was one of containment of Communism within countries controlled by the Soviet Union. Even the anti-Soviet uprisings in Hungary in 1956 and Czechoslovakia in 1968 produced no greater support than official American sympathy and the admission to the United States of refugees who had managed to reach the West.

Continued lobbying for the independence of the homeland by eastern European groups, reinforced by anti-Soviet postwar immigrants, has not aroused antagonistic reactions from the public generally, partly because of shared anti-Soviet feelings, partly because the lobbying carries no risk of producing policy likely to lead to war. Willingness to encourage or even to accept official support for a homeland cause in response to pressures from an ethnic group may change abruptly, however, if the public perceives that the costs of a previously popular cause are becoming too high. This may be the case with respect to the firm policy of American support for the state of Israel, a policy ardently promoted by Jewish-American organizations since its founding in 1948.

Until the 1970s, Jewish Americans lobbying for Israel aroused little public opposition, given the general admiration for the accomplishments of the Israeli people and their courage in defending themselves. However, as the Arab countries grew in power and increased their control over their oil resources with spiraling economic impact on the West, the advantages of establishing better relations with the Arab powers became increasingly important to Americans and the public popularity of the Israeli cause began to diminish. The erosion of virtually automatic support for Israel was marked by the failure of Jewish-American leaders, despite intensive lobbying, to prevent congressional approval in the spring of 1978 of the sale of advanced jet fighters to Egypt and Saudi Arabia.

The long debate over this issue also produced increasing resentment throughout the country over the costs to the United States of maintaining support for Israel and intimations of a reaction against Jewish Americans because of it. This threat of an era of bad feeling subsided with the accord reached at the Camp David conference of September 1978 and the signing of a peace treaty between Israel and Egypt in March 1979. However, the experience illustrates the possibility that unpopular demands by an ethnic group may produce more than a negative reaction to the policy the group seeks; it may also produce some anger and resentment against the group itself—even for causes previously popular with the public.

In one case the carry-over of ancestral quarrels has created problems for American policy toward the homelands in question and thus conflict between ethnic loyalties and the claims of U.S. national policy. Turkey's invasion of Cyprus in 1974, to aid Turkish Cypriots in their long struggle against Greek domination, provoked a move in Washington to suspend U.S. military aid to Turkey because it had violated restrictions on the use of aid for offensive purposes. This effort was strongly promoted by Greek-American organizations; the American Hellenic Institute organized a lobby in

Washington to press the issue and two Greek-American congressmen, Paul Sarbannes of Maryland and John Brademas of Indiana, successfully led action to place an embargo on aid to Turkey in 1975. The embargo, and especially the Greek-American lobbying for it, caused great resentment among Turkish Americans, who mounted a countercampaign through the Federation of Turkish American Societies to have the aid to Turkey restored. The president pressed for repeal of the embargo, claiming that U.S. security required that Turkey remain militarily strong, and Congress lifted the embargo in 1978. In spite of the president's position, opposition to repeal, especially from Greek Americans, was strong enough to make the restoration of aid conditional on proof of Turkey's good faith in reducing tensions on the Cyprus issue.

Foreign Lobbying

Resentment against ethnic groups lobbying for the homeland is most likely to arise when a group appears to be acting as agent for the government of the homeland rather than out of its own feelings of loyalty toward the home country. This was the situation in the 1920s and 1930s when Mussolini's government carried on extensive propaganda efforts among Italian Americans to build official good will for Italy. The deliberate nature of the campaign and the widespread enthusiasm for Mussolini among Italian Americans provoked public concern—and also conflict within the Italian-American community between supporters and opponents of Mussolini. When the United States declared war in 1941, however, Italian-American support for Mussolini ended and there was little retribution directed against Italians in the United States during the war.

Hitler's government also made attempts to organize German Americans to promote sympathy for Nazi Germany in the United States. The German American response was slight, but the intense anti-German feelings from World War I aroused official suspicion and investigation of such organizations soon after their founding. None was able to sustain activity for more than a few years. The Friends of the New Germany, formed in 1933, collapsed in 1935 under investigation by the House Committee on Immigration and Naturalization; the German American Bund, organized in 1936, was able to stage mass rallies in 1936 and 1939 in Madison Square Garden but was weakened by the investigation by the House Un-American Activities Committee in 1938. It disbanded in 1939 when its principal organizer, Fritz Julius Kuhn, was convicted of embezzling its funds.

The government of Portugal in the early 1960s carried the appeal of the homeland to its American ethnic constituency to new lengths and aroused both public and official resentment. Portugal, which had lost its colonies in India and faced the beginnings of serious revolt in Angola, wished to promote American good will. The government of Prime Minister António de Oliveira Salazar employed a New York public-relations firm to stimulate Portuguese-American organizations to put pressure on the U.S. government to support Portuguese policies in Africa. These efforts were investigated as illegal lobbying for a foreign government by the Senate Committee on Foreign Relations in 1963.

Similarly, attempts by the government of Korea, carried out through the Korean Central Intelligence Agency, to influence U.S. policy were exposed in congressional investigations in 1977 and 1978. The exposures created a climate of suspicion and hostility potentially threatening to Korean Americans, whether they sympathized with the Korean government or not.

An unusual episode of direct appeal to the American public by foreign leaders took the form of virtual political campaigning in the United States by Egyptian President Anwar Sadat and Prime Minister Menachem Begin of Israel in the months preceding the Camp David conference of 1978. The U.S. government was acting as an unofficial mediator in the dispute, and further it could influence the bargaining process toward a peace agreement through the extension or withholding of various forms of U.S. aid to the two parties. Both leaders, therefore, sought to ensure and enlarge the favor of Washington in the negotiations, and did so partly by appealing to their respective ethnic groups and other supporters in the United States to urge the cause of the homeland directly to the American president or through congressional representatives. During this unusually direct engagement of foreign leaders with the American public, there was little evidence of resentment or recrimination directed at them or at the ethnic sympathizers to whom they appealed.

Relations with Hostile or Enemy Homelands

The difficulty of balancing dual affinities and loyalties becomes acute when relations between the ethnic homeland and the United States are tense, hostile, or worse, when the two nations are at war. Members of ethnic groups are forced to choose between hostility toward the homeland and hostility toward the United States, or to attempt against all odds to represent the homeland interest to the American public and government in the hope of changing attitudes from hostility to sympathy.

The experience of ethnic groups caught in this dilemma reveals, more than any other aspect of the experience of dual loyalty, the intensity of feeling that surrounds the question of loyalty, the strong emotional dimension of the bond between individual and nation. In times of tension and trouble, the spirit of tolerance that normally permits the open discussion of homeland interests quickly dissipates and is replaced by an aura of suspicion through which questions and differences tend to be perceived as threats and the questioners as enemies.

The response of American ethnic groups to these pressures, especially in the extreme case of war, has been to suspend their sense of connection to the homeland and to act in accordance with their primary loyalty to the United States. The number of people who have refused to support an American war effort out of loyalty to the homeland has been extremely small. It has been more common for ethnic groups whose homelands have become unfriendly to U.S. interests to dissociate themselves from homeland policies. For example, in 1941 a group of prominent Irish Americans, incensed with Ireland's policy of neutrality in the face of full-scale European war, attempted to convince the Irish government to set aside its traditional hostility toward England and join the Allies in their fight against Nazi Germany. It was an unsuccessful effort, but noteworthy in the ordering of loyalties it expressed.

The most devastating experience of an ethnic group that tried to promote an unpopular homeland cause was that of German Americans during World War I. They attempted through their ethnic organizations to present the German point of view to Americans well beyond the time when public sympathy had turned distinctly anti-German. The major vehicle for pro-German sentiment was the National German-American Alliance (1901–1918), a cultural organization devoted before the war to such diverse causes as promoting the teaching of German and fighting Prohibition. With an impressive membership of approximately 2 million people in 1914, the alliance during the early years of the war sponsored mass demonstrations, collected German war-relief funds, lobbied for embargoes on loans and the sale of arms to England, promoted the sale of Imperial war bonds, and campaigned for the defeat of Woodrow Wilson in the presidential election of 1916. The German-American press, which included over 500

German-language publications, was also virtually unanimous in its pro-German sentiment and its insistence on American neutrality.

Joined by Irish Americans in opposition to U.S. entry into the war on the side of England and by millions of Americans without ethnic bonds to the belligerents but who opposed any American involvement in European affairs, German Americans could express antiwar sentiments in 1914 and 1915 with little fear of public resentment. Anti-German sentiment began to grow, however, as the war wore on and particularly as German attacks on merchant ships carrying civilian passengers intensified

When the United States finally entered the war in 1917, German Americans and their organizations, churches, places of business, and cultural connections generally became the objects of furious attack. Anti-German fervor brought about the boycott of music composed by Germans, the renaming of places with German names, arrests of German Americans for unpatriotic speech, and the elimination or restriction of German-language instruction in schools. The virulence of public attitudes toward German Americans for their prewar loyalty to the homeland resulted in the rapid, often permanent, collapse of German ethnic associations. The National German-American Alliance dissolved under Senate investigation; by 1920 the number of German-language publications had dropped to half the number circulating in 1910; most local German-American organizations erased their ethnic identity.

The postwar political turbulence in Germany, followed by Hitler's attainment of power in 1933 and then World War II, made it all but impossible to express a sense of kinship with Germany. German Americans have never reestablished a strong associational life based on their ethnic bonds. Of the more than 200 German-language publications that survived World War I, only 24 remained in 1976.

Greek Americans suffered a similar fate in the aftermath of World War I. The neutrality of Greece during the war, combined with the strong German ties of the Greek royal family, created a stigma which made open expression of attachment to the homeland a rarity in the Greek-American community. In 1940, however, the resistance of the Greeks to Italy's invasion of their country made links to the homeland once more a source of pride for Greek Americans.

In the immediate postwar years, disillusion with the outcome of World War I and a general reaction against European influences in American life fed a resurgence of nativist attitudes that produced, among other things, the restrictive immigration laws of 1921 and 1924, but also acute concern about foreign subversion of U.S. politics—the Red Scare. Russian Americans, especially socialists and other radicals enthusiastic about the Bolshevik Revolution in 1917, were the primary objects of suspicion and retribution. In New York City, approximately 5,000 people were arrested in raids on the headquarters of the Union of Russian Workers in 1919 and of the Russian-dominated American Communist party in 1920. Anti-Russian feeling, first aroused by the Russian Revolution but sustained by continued hostility toward Russian Communism, has produced an assimilationist reaction among Russian Americans similar to that of German Americans since World War I. Out of fear of social or even official retribution, Russian Americans have played down their ethnic identity and allowed many of their ethnic associations to lapse.

The most repressive antiethnic reaction to the enemy status of the homeland was the internment of Japanese Americans during World War II. On February 19, 1942, two months after the Japanese attack on Pearl Harbor, Executive Order 9066 authorized the removal of "dangerous persons" from areas along the Pacific Coast and their internment in government camps in the interior. By August 1942 nearly 120,000 Japanese, 64 percent of them U.S. citizens, were moved from their homes to the camps, where most of them had to stay until the end of the war.

The military logic of the order was to counter the possibility of Japanese Americans giving secret aid to the Japanese war effort, including possibly facilitating an attack on the West Coast. There was, however, little evidence of such subversive activity or, after the outbreak of war, of the prevalence among Japanese Americans of pro-Japanese sentiments that might make military subversion a risk. Even military leaders did not agree about the need for internment as a security measure.

Pressure for the relocation of Japanese Americans came primarily from the public in California, where anti-Japanese attitudes had taken various legislative forms since the late 19th century and had been suddenly intensified by identification of the group with an actual, external enemy. In the Japanese experience, more than that of any other group, the accusation of group disloyalty was a function of prejudice, of the intolerance of difference within American society.

Similar reactions occurred in official attitudes toward Chinese Americans after the Communist revolution had converted China from an ally to a Cold War enemy in 1949, attitudes that hardened when the Chinese entered the Korean War and became enemies on a battlefield. Concern in the mid-1950s about the illegal entry into the United States of Chinese through Hong Kong, together with suspicion about the ties and loyalties of Chinese Americans to the homeland, produced a plan for the deportation of thousands of Chinese from the United States. Intensive lobbying by the National Chinese Welfare Council forestalled the deportations, but official and public suspicion toward Chinese Americans remained alive, especially in California, and began to dissipate only with United States initiatives toward normal relations with China in the early 1970s.

Exceptions to Exceptionalism

Wilson was not alone, during the American age of innocence, in conceiving of the United States as a unique entity, as a "great ideal" that transcended and thus could unite nations. The assumption was widespread, when the United States was relatively isolated from world affairs, that Americans could be free from the old nationalisms which divided humanity into the enclaves Wilson called "jealous camps." For the new nation, the old terms of national loyalty would not apply because national divisions would be recognized as ultimately meaningless, matters of administrative convenience only. Citizens of the United States, Wilson had said, owed their first loyalty to humanity. Under this conception of the nation, problems of dual loyalty would not arise.

Although the ideal of the neutral nation, the nation without national interest and nationalist spirit, has not been fully realized since Wilson's time, neither has it been wholly irrelevant to the actual experience of the United States.

Beginning with its entry into World War I, the United States has been drawn into close, constant relations with the other centers of world power and inevitably has had to conduct these relations as a nation dealing with other nations. U.S. relations with others have been variously friendly, hostile, peaceful or warring, and the American people have responded to these conditions with traditionally patriotic attitudes of good will for friends, condemnation for enemies. Times of war or crisis have aroused in the American public much the same sentiments of national loyalty that earlier generations of Americans had deplored in the Old World. At such times the problem of dual loyalty, or suspected divided loyalty among members of an ethnic group whose homeland is hostile to the United States, has become acute—as the experience of German, Greek, Japanese, and Russian Americans illustrates.

In the absence of crisis, however, there has been a generalized tolerance, in the spirit of Wilson's ideal, for the promotion by ethnic groups in the United States of various interests important to the homeland. Continued affection for and identification with the homeland have been generally regarded as natural, and a variety of activities supporting the homeland have come to be accepted as legitimate. However, there are limits to such activities even in times of peace. While the openness of the American political system encourages a multiplicity of interests and allows groups great leeway to act on their differences, it also sets up counterpressures to smooth out differences, even to deny them. There is greater tension in American democracy than Wilson foresaw, a greater propensity for fear of difference. As a result, American ethnic groups have experienced both extensive tolerance and extensive intolerance in reaction to their expression of their complex loyalties.

On the whole, the phenomenon of dual loyalty has not greatly influenced the relations of the United States with other nations. There has been little serious subversive activity against the United States on behalf of a group's homeland. The efforts of interested ethnic groups have had more effect instead on the establishment of friendly ties between the United States and other countries, and on the provision of U.S. aid, diplomatic or financial. However, no ethnic group has been able to promote an official policy favorable to the homeland unless it has also had a wider base of public acceptance or has carried little risk or cost to the United States.

The most serious conflict that has been created by loyalties running both to the United States and to the homeland has been the one experienced by the ethnic group itself in the process of establishing its American identity. The most important link to the homeland has been the need of each ethnic group for a source of pride and self-respect to aid it in establishing a dignified place in American society.

BIBLIOGRAPHY

2. Voting and Parties

The pioneering work on ethnocultural political theory is Lee Benson, *The Concept of Jacksonian Democracy: New York as a Test Case* (Princeton, N.J., 1961). Samuel Lubell, *The Future of American Politics*, 2d ed., rev. (Garden City, N.Y., 1955), is another pathbreaking work of a more popular character. Ronald Formisano, *The Birth of Mass Political Parties: Michigan, 1827–1861* (Princeton, N.J., 1971), follows Benson's approach, as does Richard J. Jensen, *The Winning of the Midwest: Social and Political Conflict, 1888–1896* (Chicago, 1971). Two good summaries of the ethnocultural approach are Samuel T. McSeveney, "Ethnic Groups, Ethnic Conflict, and Recent Quantitative Research in American Political History," *International Migration Review* 7 (Spring 1973): 14–33, and Robert Kelley, "Ideology and Political Culture from Jefferson to Nixon," *American History Review* 82 (1977): 531–562.

A delightful introduction to boss politics is William L. Riordon, ed., *Plunkitt of Tammany Hall* (New York, 1963). Bruce Stave, ed., *Urban Bosses, Machines, and Progressive Reformers* (Lexington, Mass., 1972), is a useful collection of articles. There are numerous studies of individual bosses and machines.

Discussions of the Irish political style appear in William V. Shannon, *The American Irish*, rev. ed. (1966, reprint, 1973), and Edward M. Levine, *The Irish and Irish Politicians* (South Bend, Ind., 1966). For the Poles, see Edward R. Kantowicz, *Polish-American Politics in Chicago* (Chicago, 1975). Three works by Frederick C. Luebke discuss the Germans: *Immigrants and Politics: The Germans of Nebraska, 1880–1900* (Lincoln, Neb., 1969); *Bonds of Loyalty: German Americans and World War I* (DeKalb, Ill., 1974); *Ethnic*

Voters and the Election of Lincoln (Lincoln, Neb., 1971). Information on Scandinavians in politics must be dug out of a variety of sources, for example: G. Theodore Mitau, *Politics in Minnesota*, 2d ed. (Minneapolis, 1970); and Kendric C. Babcock, *The Scandinavian Element in the United States* (1914; reprint, New York, 1969). Lawrence H. Fuchs, *The Political Behavior of American Jews* (Glencoe, Ill., 1956) is a standard survey. Harold Gosnell, *Negro Politicians: The Rise of Negro Politics in Chicago* (Chicago, 1935) is a standard, older work. A useful collection of recent works on many ethnic groups, including blacks, Poles, and Jews, is Peter Jones and Melvin G. Holli, eds., *The Ethnic Frontier* (Grand Rapids, Mich., 1977).

3. Leadership

John Higham, ed., *Ethnic Leadership in America* (Baltimore, 1977), contains essays on Jews by Nathan Glazer, on Afro-Americans by Nathan I. Huggins, on American Indians by Robert F. Berkhofer, Jr., on Germans by Frederick Luebke, on Japanese by Roger Daniels, on eastern and southern Europeans by Josef J. Barton, on Irish by Robert D. Cross, and on Hawaiians by John Higham. Kurt Lewin discusses "The Problem of Minority Leadership" in *Resolving Social Conflicts: Selected Papers on Group Dynamics* (New York, 1948). Gunnar Myrdal, *An American Dilemma* (New York, 1944), pt. 9, "Leadership and Concerted Action," develops in rich detail the classic distinction between protest leadership and accommodating leadership. James Q. Wilson, *Negro Politics: The Search for Leadership* (Glencoe, Ill., 1960) is a tough-minded and influential study of Chicago. Everett Carll Ladd, Jr., *Negro Political Leadership in the South* (Ithaca, N.Y., 1966), confirms and further develops Wilson's thesis in a very different setting. Melvin G. Holli and Peter d'A. Jones, eds., *The Ethnic Frontier: Essays in the History of Group Survival in Chicago and the Midwest* (Grand Rapids, Mich., 1977), contains several relevant essays, especially Victor Greene, "'Becoming American': The Role of Ethnic Leaders—Swedes, Poles, Italians, Jews." Daniel J. Elazar, *Community and Polity: The Organizational Dynamics of American Jewry* (Philadelphia, 1976), is a penetrating analysis of the structure of internal leadership. Nicholas

Tavuchis, *Pastors and Immigrants: The Role of a Religious Elite in the Absorption of Norwegian Immigrants* (The Hague, 1963), is a socio-logical study of received leadership in the mid-19th century. Timothy L. Smith, "Lay Initiative in the Religious Life of American Immigrants, 1880–1950," in *Anonymous Americans: Explorations in Nineteenth-Century Social History*, Tamara K. Hareven, ed. (Engle-wood Cliffs, N.J., 1971), should be compared with Alan Graebner, *Uncertain Saints: The Laity in the Lutheran Church–Missouri Synod, 1900–1970* (Westport, Conn., 1975).

4. Loyalties: Dual and Divided

The only comprehensive book on the topic is Louis L. Gerson, *The Hyphenate in Recent American Politics and Diplomacy* (Lawrence, Kans., 1964), which provides a well-documented review of the engagement of ethnic groups in homeland issues from the late 19th century.

John Higham, *Strangers in the Land: Patterns of American Nativism, 1860–1925* (New York, 1973), is a rich and sensitive study of attitudes toward foreignness in general; chapters 8 and 9 deal with the experience of German Americans during World War I and the postwar Red Scare.

Thomas N. Brown, *Irish-American Nationalism, 1870–1890* (Phil-adelphia, 1966), is a perceptive examination of the sources of immigrant nationalism; his thesis is applicable to other ethnic groups as well. This connection is specifically drawn in an elegant essay by Maldwyn A. Jones, *The Old World Ties of American Ethnic Groups* (London, 1976).

Informative studies of specific ethnic-group issues of broad political significance include: Roger Daniel, *Concentration Camps U.S.A.: Japanese Americans and World War II* (New York, 1972), especially its review of the way in which the evacuation decision was made; Samuel Halperin, *The Political World of American Zion-ism* (Detroit, 1964), a detailed history of the movement and its opponents up to 1945; Robert Silverberg, *If I Forget Thee O Jerusalem: American Jews and the State of Israel* (New York, 1970), a detailed but undocumented journalistic account of the involvement of Jew-ish Americans in promoting the cause of Israel through 1969; John

P. Diggin, *Mussolini and Fascism: The View from America* (Princeton, N.J., 1972), which includes two informative chapters on the reactions of Italian Americans to Fascism in Italy; and Robert G. Weisbord, *Ebony Kinship: Africa, Africans, and the Afro-American* (Westport, Conn., 1973), which traces the correspondence in attitudes black Americans have held toward Africa and toward themselves.